POWER TO LOVE

Yours in Christ

Cecil Kerr.

EPHESIANS 3 V 14-21.

Surely you know you are God's temple and that God's Spirit lives in you. So if anyone destroys God's temple God will destroy him. For God's temple is holy, and you, yourselves are his temple. No one should fool himself. If anyone among you, should think he is a wise man by this world's standards he should become a fool, in order to be really wise. For what this world considers to be wise is nonsense. You belong to Christ and Christ belongs to God.

POWER TO LOVE

Christian Renewal and Reconciliation

by
CECIL KERR

CHRISTIAN JOURNALS LIMITED
BELFAST

First edition 1976 by Christian Journals Limited,
2 Bristow Park, Belfast BT9 6TH

Cover by TREVOR ANDREWS
ISBN 0 904302 17 2

Made and printed in Ireland

Contents

For he is our peace, who has made us both one, and has broken down the dividing wall of hostility.

Ephesians 2 v. 14

Preface

I have written this book out of a very real conviction that God is doing a 'new thing' in our world to-day and especially here in Ireland. Miraculously in this war-torn land

> Old walls are falling down
> And men are speaking with each other.

One morning in the very early spring our postman was walking up the path towards one of the houses on his round. During the winter a solid coat of tarmacadam had been laid along the path. That morning he noticed a little bulge in the tarmac and thought it must be water forcing its way from underneath. A few days later he discovered the real cause. Pushing its way through that dark unfriendly surface was a little crocus reaching its leaves towards the spring sunshine. To me that simple incident is a parable for our land. Through the awful tragedy which we have known and despite the terrible terror which we have experienced a new hope is being born. As men and women turn to the Living God in repentance and faith a new way is being opened through the hard soil of hatred and bitterness into the light of a new day of hope and brotherhood. It is my firm belief that only through faith in Christ can this land be saved from a terrible future. What I have to say is primarily addressed to all who profess to follow Christ. A terrible responsibility is placed on us to be what we profess to be.

Earlier this year in Rome I had the privilege of meeting a young Arab Christian—a member of a small prayer group in Israel! She said to me: 'We often think of Ireland and pray for you. If God can heal Ireland then we believe He can do something for the Middle East.' Never before has there been such a challenge to the Christian Church in the world. I believe it is a difficult but exciting time to be a Christian. With the Prior of Taizé I believe 'the Risen Christ comes to quicken a festival in the innermost heart of man. He is preparing a spring time of the Church for us, a Church devoid of means of power, ready to share with all, a place of visible communion for all humanity. He is going to give us enough imagination and courage to open up a path of reconciliation. He is going to prepare us to give our life so that man be no longer victim of man'.

God is calling us out beyond the perimeters which we have set ourselves. In this book I am saying nothing new. It is my desire to attempt to 'hear what the Spirit is saying to the Churches' in this critical time. I have deliberately drawn attention to Scripture and the passages which I have quoted will repay careful study. May we not only hear these words but also obey them.

I wish to thank Myrtle, my wife, for her great patience and encouragement; my colleagues at the Christian Renewal Centre for their prayerful support; Lavinia Bowerman for the cheerful and efficient way in which she typed the manuscript and finally the Rev. Wilbert Forker of Christian Journals Limited for all his help and advice.

CECIL KERR

Rostrevor
Christmas 1975

1. "If My People . . ."

It was a beautiful Saturday in early Summer. The tree clad mountains of Mourne sweeping down to the shores of Carlingford Lough provided a perfect backdrop for the coloured sails of the yachts taking part in the local regatta. All afternoon a fresh breeze had sent those boats skimming over the crystal water giving obvious joy to the yachtsmen and spectators. Then in the early evening the wind on the Lough suddenly dropped and those boats sat becalmed, only inching their way towards the finishing line. As I reflected on that scene just across the road from the Christian Renewal Centre I realized what a parable it was of our Churches today. Those boats were well equipped, they were beautifully painted, their sails were trimmed and their crews were on board. One essential was missing —the wind to take them to the finishing line. The Irish skyline is dotted with the towers and spires of Churches. On almost every corner of our city streets there are Church buildings. Where we lived in Belfast there were four Church buildings in our avenue. In the new housing estates that mushroom round our developing cities new Churches are conspicuous among the rows of houses and the blocks of flats. The Churches are well furnished and still in many cases well filled. Though there is a growing shortage of clergy in all the Churches there is still an abundance of manpower. What has gone wrong ?

The non-Christian observer of the Irish scene today can be excused when he asks the question 'Why is it that there is so much hatred and violence in a country which professes so much Christianity ?' It is a question which one is asked with embarrassing regularity when one travels in Europe and abroad. It was the historian Lecky who over one hundred years ago observed: "If the characteristic mark of a healthy Christianity be to unite its members by a bond of fraternity and love, there is no country in the world in which Christianity has more completely failed than in Ireland.'

Time and time again over the past six years those words have been illustrated by the awful prejudice, fear and bigotry which has erupted in such demonic violence across our land. Ireland once known as the land of 'saints and scholars' has become a dark blot on the map of the Christian world and a byeword among the nations.

There is no doubt in my mind that we are facing in Ireland today the greatest spiritual crisis that this country has ever faced in its long history. The battle is joined for the 'soul' of Ireland and behind the physical violence a far more subtle spiritual warfare is being fought. Terrible demonic forces have been unleashed which drive man against man and brother against brother. Behind the daily atrocities which fill the newspaper headlines the words of St. Paul in his letter to the Ephesians are very relevant and real.

> For we are not contending against flesh and blood, but against the principalities, against the powers, against the world rulers of this present darkness, against the spiritual hosts of wickedness in the heavenly places.
>
> Ephesians 6 v. 12

St. Paul goes on to give advice about how to meet these forces.

10

> Therefore take the whole armour of God, that you may be able to withstand in the evil day, and having done all, to stand. Stand therefore, having girded your loins with truth, and having put on the breastplate of righteousness, and having shod your feet with the equipment of the gospel of peace; besides all these, taking the shield of faith, with which you can quench all the flaming darts of the evil one. And take the helmet of salvation, and the sword of the Spirit, which is the word of God. Pray at all times in the Spirit, with all prayer and supplication. To that end keep alert with all perseverance, making supplication for all the saints.
>
> Ephesians 6 vs. 13-18

As the darkness deepens in our land and in the world there are many who fear it, some who curse it and others who analyse it. Christians are called to be reflectors of the light of Christ in the darkness of the world. 'You are the light of the world,' said Jesus to his disciples, 'a city set on a hill cannot be hid.' Christ's parting promise to the disciples was this 'Peace I leave with you.'

> I have said this to you, that in me you may have peace. In the world you have tribulation; but be of good cheer, I have overcome the world.
>
> Saint John 16 v. 33

As the Christian Church is renewed in the love of Christ and in the power of the Holy Spirit this land can become a visual aid to the rest of the world of the healing power of the love of God. A pre-requisite of that renewal is repentance.

There is surely more than a grain of truth in the words of William Cowper:

> When nations are to perish in their sins
> 'Tis in the Church the leprosy begins.

11

'Judgement must begin at the house of God' and I believe He is speaking in judgement to His people today.

Over the past few years a text of Scripture has come home to me with great urgency in relation to the situation in which we find ourselves. It is the word of God spoken to Solomon three thousand years ago but I believe it enshrines some abiding principles. Solomon had just finished the building of the great Temple in Jerusalem. The Chronicles tells us that 'all that Solomon had planned to do in the house of the Lord and in his own house he successfully accomplished'. After the excitement of the dedication of that magnificent building as Solomon lay awake in the night God spoke to him and said :

> When I shut up the heavens so that there is no rain, or command the locust to devour the land, or send pestilence among my people, if my people who are called by my name humble themselves, and pray and seek my face, and turn from their wicked ways, then I will hear from heaven, and will forgive their sin and heal their land.

2 Chronicles 7 vs. 13-14

The onus is on 'the people of God'. They are those who have the responsibility to meet God's conditions when disaster strikes. There are f o u r conditions which God's people are asked to fulfill : (i) to humble ourselves; (ii) to pray; (iii) to seek God's face and (iv) to turn from our wicked ways. When we meet these four conditions God makes three promises : (i) to hear from heaven; (ii) to forgive our sin and (iii) to heal our land. It is important to notice that these conditions are binding not on the violent, evil and godless people but on God's people. It is so easy to put the blame onto someone else and in the churches in Ireland we are in danger of excusing ourselves and self righteously disassociating ourselves from the 'men of violence'. God calls us to much more positive action. I remember once hearing Dr. Martin Niemöller speak and I was struck by his great humility. He said something to this effect: 'I was a member of the Christian Church in the Germany in which Hitler came to power and Nazism grew.' He acknowledged his responsibility and that of other Christians for the ways in which they allowed evil to grow.

We in Ireland cannot deny the support that has so often been given to bigotry in the name of Christianity. One perceptive commentator has observed that in Ireland 'we have secularized our Christianity and sacrilized our politics'. For this God calls us to deep repentance. Time and time again in the history of the people of Israel the prophets recalled them to the basic demands of God, pointing out that all their religious observance was useless, indeed abhorrent if their hearts were not right and their hands were not clean in relation to their neighbours.

> I hate, I despise your feasts, and I take no delight in your solemn assemblies. Even though you offer me your burnt offerings and cereal offerings, I will not accept them, and the peace offerings of your fatted beasts I will not look upon. Take away from me the noise of your songs; to the melody of your harps I will not listen. But let justice roll down like waters, and righteousness like an ever-flowing stream.
>
> Amos 5 vs. 21-24

In a situation remarkably like our own God's Word came to a very sensitive man called Jeremiah in the sixth century before Christ. Around him he felt the impending doom that was coming upon his people and he lived to share in the horrors of war and famine which destroyed Jerusalem in 586 B.C. With clear insight he declared the heart of the problem.

13

For my people have committed two evils: they have forsaken me, the fountain of living waters, and hewed out cisterns for themselves, broken cisterns, that can hold no water.

Jeremiah 2 v. 13

For my people are foolish, they know me not; they are stupid children, they have no understanding. They are skilled in doing evil, but how to do good they know not.

Deeply sensitive to the terrible violence and treachery which surrounded him he cried :

O that my head were waters, and my eyes a fountain of tears, that I might weep day and night for the slain of the daughter of my people! O that I had in the desert a wayfarers' lodging place, that I might leave my people and go away from them! For they are all adulterers, a company of treacherous men. They bend their tongue like a bow; falsehood and not truth has grown strong in the land; for they proceed from evil to evil, and they do not know me, says the Lord. Let every one beware of his neighbour, and put no trust in any brother; for every brother is a supplanter, and every neighbour goes about as a slanderer. Every one deceives his neighbour, and no one speaks the truth; they have taught their tongue to speak lies; they commit iniquity and are too weary to repent. Heaping oppression upon oppression, and deceit upon deceit, they refuse to know me, says the Lord. Therefore thus says the Lord of hosts: Behold I will refine them and test them, for what else can I do, because of my people? Their tongue is a deadly arrow; it speaks deceitfully; with his mouth each speaks peaceably to his neighbour, but in his heart he plans an ambush for him. Shall I not punish them for these things? says the Lord; and shall I not avenge myself on a nation such as this?

Jeremiah 9 vs. 1-9

Who is the man so wise that he can understand this? To whom has the mouth of the Lord spoken, that he may declare it? Why is the land ruined and laid waste like a wilderness, so that no one passes through? And the Lord says: Because they have forsaken my law which I set before them, and have not obeyed my voice, or walked in accord with it.

Jeremiah 9 vs. 12 & 13

Over the past few years we have heard much talk about renewal in many of the Churches. The tragedy is that it is so often 'man made', the result of our deliberations, our schemes and our programmes. I am sure that many of us who have served on Church committees concerned with renewal would echo the words of the theologian Charles Davis when he wrote:

> Much speaking in different places on themes of renewal has brought me into contact with many people seeking to revivify their faith. I have found a sense of emptiness, but together with it a deep yearning for God. There is an emptiness at the core of people's lives, an emptiness waiting to be filled. They are troubled about their faith; they find it slipping. I am not speaking of those who are worried about recent changes. These people are not. But they are looking for something more; they are looking for something to fill the void in their lives, and what they hear does not do that. The more perceptive know they are looking for God. He seems to have withdrawn

15

from the world and from them. They come to talks by speakers like myself. They hear about the new liturgy, about the new understanding of the layman's role, about collegiality, about the Church and the world, about a thousand and one new and exciting ideas. They are duly impressed. But who will speak to them quite simply of God as of a person he intimately knows, and make the reality and presence of God alive for them once more?

Before such need, how superficial, pathetically superficial, is much of the busyness with renewal. We reformers know so much about religion and about the Church and about theology, but we stand empty-handed and uncomfortable when confronted with sheer hunger for God.[1]

The truth of these words could be illustrated by countless men and women today. A friend of mine, a Roman Catholic priest, related his experience. Involved as a priest in a very busy city parish in America he was becoming more and more frustrated and disillusioned in his ministry. One day a young hippie came to see him 'high on heroin'. My friend, Father Joe showed the boy into a room and sat down. The boy looked at Father Joe out of his bloodshot eyes and said: 'Please tell me that there is something to live for or I'll kill myself. I feel like there is a great block of concrete over my head and there's no way out.' Father Joe just looked at him and he had no answer that he could honestly give that boy. Then the boy said: 'Please pray for me,' and Father Joe couldn't pray. Then the boy himself prayed a simple prayer. 'Jesus Christ, if you are real, reveal yourself to me.' In a few minutes Father Joe said that boy stood up and it was obvious something had happened to him, his prayer was answered. Over the next three weeks that boy just grew stronger in his faith in Christ and many of his friends began to call. They saw the change in him and he witnessed to the power of Christ to change them too. Father Joe told me that what he saw happening brought him to his knees and he prayed 'Lord Jesus Christ, let me know with a deep assurance that you are my Lord and Saviour.' Christ answered his prayer too and baptized Father Joe in the Holy Spirit and today he is reaching many people, young and old, with the message of Christ's love and power.

It has become increasingly clear to me especially after spending nine years as a University Chaplain that formal, institutionalized Christianity will have little effect in the world today. I believe in Ireland we have seen the last generation of conventional Christians—those who go to Church because it is the thing to do. The future Church will be composed of those who really believe what they profess.

Father Michael Paul Gallagher, a lecturer in English in University College, Dublin, has drawn attention to a fact of Irish life, North and South, Catholic and Protestant which we ignore at our peril. Writing out of a wide experience of working with young people both within the University and outside it he says:

> What I have found is that the bottom has fallen out of conventional faith for many of this age group. What their parents believe and practise sincerely as religion has turned them off. What they are taught as religion in school has gradually bored and even embittered them. What they experience for the most part in Church on Sunday is a dull ritual that does not express anything meaningful for them. The result is that their image of Church and faith is not something worth growing into. So they 'lose faith', or

17

perhaps more accurately they lose hope that what is presented as 'the faith' could ever again come alive in their lives. Very many may continue to practise with these doubts and reservations and sense of uninvolvement. Others will quietly decide not to practise. Others again will become quite explicit in their rejection of all that religion stands for.[2]

From my experience of young people from a Protestant background I would endorse what he has said. So many brought up in the Protestant tradition have been 'immunized' by a dose of Christianity. It is a sad fact but true that in many Churches confirmation becomes the 'passing out parade' instead of a 'signing on for active service'. Ralph Martin in his book *Unless the Lord build the House* points to a similar deficiency in the Roman Catholic tradition when he says :

The saving message, the kerygma, has not been effectively understood or appropriated by the Church as a whole. Countless millions of baptized Catholics in this country and others, have not personally committed their lives to Jesus, accepting him as their Saviour and Lord. Nor do they, despite the sacrament of confirmation, experience the effective power and working of the Holy Spirit in their lives. To sacramentalize or catechize in a situation like this can only produce a misshapen Christianity.[3]

These are facts which stare us in the face as Christians today and we cannot ignore their challenge if we are to present a wholesome Christian faith to the rising generation. These young people are part of a 'questioning generation'. They have been taught since kindergarten to probe, to search and to explore. They can very quickly cut through the hypocrisy which masquerades as reality and ask the awkward questions. They also belong to a feeling generation; they want to 'experience' not just to know in an intellectual way. And this again has sprung largely from the revolution in primary education. In the primary school the child is introduced into a world of experiencing the environment in which he lives and participating with others in exploring that environment.

At the heart of Christianity is an experience. God can be known by faith in Christ who comes to live within us in a real and experiential way. Helping people to this awareness of Christ's indwelling power and presence is surely the primary task of the Church in this day and age. Later in the article from which I have already quoted, Father Gallagher has this to say :

> Too much emphasis has been put in the past on religion as involving obedience to specific activities and practices. In a new culture that kind of practice cannot continue without internal conviction. So the pastoral focus has to change from being content with continuity of practice to preparing for more explicit commitment of faith. Up to now much teaching and preaching seemed to assume that continuity of practice was possible and sufficient. It was never sufficient and in our new situation it may not be possible either, unless rooted in some adult conversion. In many cases the young people who are rejecting Church practice may not be rejecting Christ at all, for the simple reason that they may never have experienced him as real or as the living Lord.

What I have been trying to say has been very well expressed by a French priest, Michel Quoist, in his stimulating book *Christ is alive*. Michael Quoist has touched a generation of young people in a remarkable way through his *Prayers of Life* which pulsate with the reality of Christ's living power in the world of everyday. Writing of man's great need for God expressed in a thousand different ways in the literature of our day and in the reckless behaviour of so many people who seek some meaning in life Quoist challenges the Christian Church to reveal the 'living Christ' to a world that has lost its way. He says we must show that Christ is 'not a caricature, and not a corpse', but warns that 'our contemporaries will discover Christ in his overwhelming truth only if we, as Christians have truly encountered him ourselves'. He goes on :

> In the contemporary Church there are constant meetings and conferences, composed of bishops, priests, religious, and laymen, the purpose of which is to study, discuss, and research the best means of evangelising modern man. There are sessions, innumerable committees, staff personnel, and new structures constantly being created. There are innovators offering new ideas, techniques, and revolutionary methods. There are conservatives trying to apply the brakes, and there are militants defending the cause of 'progress' and change. This is all very well. It is even necessary. But we must ask ourselves what the source is of all this activity. Is it a more intimate contact with Christ, which is itself the result of more frequent and extended contacts? Is it primarily not the defence of methods, or research, or organisation and structures, or ideas and even dogma, rather than a great love, a 'passion' for someone—for Jesus Christ as contemplated in his mystical and historical dimensions? Are our most militant revolutionaries and our most steadfast contestants those who are most intimate with and most enthusiastic for

Christ? For that must be the criterion against which we measure the authenticity of their work. 'Make sure that no one traps you and deprives you of your freedom by some secondhand, empty, rational philosophy based on the principles of this world instead of on Christ. In his body lives the fullness of divinity' (Colossians 2 vs. 8-9).

Among all those people who gather to study and decide 'priorities', to organise the preaching of Christ—for everyone says that that is what it is all about—how many are there who do, in fact, preach Christ? And how much time is there left for them to get started on that all-important work ?

Is there anyone left who preaches Christ instead of discussing the methodology of preaching Christ ? Is there anyone left among us who, because he has met Christ and lives with him and has daily been transformed by him in the Gospel and in life, can preach his discovery, his certitude, his love, instead of mumbling words that are full of excuses ?

The desire to change and progress within the Church is indeed praiseworthy. But we are running the risk of ignoring the only thing that is essential. In our desire to make improvements, it is not impossible that we are smothering the Spirit of Christ under a fabric woven of our subtle thoughts, our organisations, tactics, and techniques. It is possible that, as we sit weaving our splendid plans for the future, our contemporaries are dying of hunger in their search for a living Person, a Saviour.[4]

The great need of the Christian Church in this hour is surely to hear God's word of judgement on us His people. To hear His word and to obey it. Too many of us are 'at ease in Zion' and blame the trouble on 'others'. As I read the Bible it occurs to me time and time again that the greater judgement is on those who have known God's word, have heard Him speak and have ignored it. How often our Lord rebuked the Scribes and Pharisees of his day, indeed his strongest language was reserved for those because they refused 'to hear' and they would not 'see'. It was our Lord's experience and St. Paul's too that those who should have known God's word, those who should have been alert to what He was doing all around them were so bound in their traditions that they could not perceive what God was doing. With great sorrow and with tears in His eyes the Lord looked out over Jerusalem, the city of a thousand privileges and He cried :

> O Jerusalem, Jerusalem, killing the prophets and stoning those who are sent to you! How often would I have gathered your children together as a hen gathers her brood under her wings, and you would not! Behold your house is forsaken and desolate.
>
> Saint Matthew 23 vs. 37 & 38

Just before that He had said:

> Woe to you, scribes and Pharisees, hypocrites ! for you are like whitewashed tombs, which outwardly appear beautiful, but within they are full of dead men's bones and all uncleanness. So you also outwardly appear righteous to men, but within you are full of hypocrisy and iniquity.
>
> Saint Matthew 23 vs. 27 & 28

It is so perilously easy for the Church to fall into the self-righteousness of the Pharisee and the correctness of the scribe. The Pharisees thought they had it all wrapped up, no one could teach them. The Scribes had it written and every jot and tittle should be kept. How easily the good can become the enemy of the best and we lock our-selves in our hermetically sealed theological systems and ecclesiastical hot houses. How tragically true it is of so many Churches that we are 'sound but sound asleep', we are 'right but dead right'. It often seems to me that God's message to the Church at Laodicea has more than a little relevance to us especially in Ireland today.

> I know your works: you are neither cold nor hot. Would that you were cold or hot! So, because you are lukewarm, and neither cold nor hot, I will spew you out of my mouth. For you say, I am rich, I have prospered, and I need nothing; not knowing that you are wretched, pitiable, poor, blind, and naked. Therefore I counsel you to buy from me gold refined by fire, that you may be rich, and white garments to clothe you and to keep the shame of your naked-ness from being seen, and salve to anoint your eyes, that you may see. Those whom I love, I reprove and chasten; so be zealous and repent. Behold, I stand at the door and knock; if any one hears my voice and opens the door, I will come in to him and eat with him, and he with me. He who conquers, I will grant him to sit with me on my throne, as I myself conquered and sat down with my Father on his throne. He who has an ear, let him hear what the Spirit says to the Churches.

Revelation 3 vs. 15-22

Because God loves His Church He chastens and reproves us. His judgement is always tempered with mercy so that we might be purged and prepared ready to fulfil His purpose in the world. It is so easy to fall into a groove and the only difference between a groove and a grave is the depth. He wants to raise us out of the sleep of death to experience the new life that His Spirit can bring. He 'who makes all things new' is the one who stands at the door of the Church and knocks. He wants to come into every corner, into every person and fill it with His life and light.

We have seen how God's judgement was pronounced upon the people of Israel when they turned away from God. It was in the depths of despair when all hope seemed gone and they appeared to be resigned to endless exile that God's word of hope broke into the darkness. It was a word of restoration and renewal. Ezekiel was the man God used to bring that vision of restoration. His words come down to us along the corridors of history to inspire us with a new vision of what God is wanting to do in our day as the Church of Christ is open to the renewing power of God's Spirit.

> The hand of the Lord was upon me, and he brought me out by the Spirit of the Lord, and set me down in the midst of the valley; it was full of bones. And he led me round among them; and behold, there were very many upon the valley; and lo, they were very dry. And he said to me, Son of man, can these bones live ? And I answered, O Lord God, thou knowest. Again he said to me, Prophesy to these bones, and say to them, O dry bones, hear the word of the Lord. Thus says the Lord God to these bones: Behold, I will cause breath to enter you, and you shall live. And I will lay sinews upon you, and will cause flesh to come upon you, and cover you with skin, and put breath in you, and you shall live; and you shall know that I am the Lord. So I prophesied as I was commanded; and as I prophesied, there was a noise, and behold, a rattling; and the bones came together, bone to its bone. And as I looked, there were sinews on them, and flesh had come upon them, and skin

covered them; but there was no breath in them. Then he said to me, Prophesy to the breath, prophesy, son of man, and say to the breath, Thus says the Lord God: Come from the four winds, O breath, and breathe upon these slain, that they may live. So I prophesied as he commanded me, and the breath came into them, and they lived, and stood upon their feet, an exceedingly great host.

Then he said to me, Son of man, these bones are the whole house of Israel. Behold, they say, Our bones are dried up, and our hope is lost; we are clean cut off. Therefore prophesy, and say to them, Thus says the Lord God: Behold, I will open your graves, and raise you from your graves, O my people; and I will bring you home into the land of Israel. And you shall know that I am the Lord, when I open your graves, and raise you from your graves, O my people. And I will put my Spirit within you, and you shall live, and I will place you in your own land; then you shall know that I, the Lord, have spoken, and I have done it, says the Lord.

Ezekiel 37 vs. 1-14

In this remarkable vision is enshrined the basic principle of God's renewing power. It is that God's Spirit alone can bring life. Notice that in the first stage of the vision Ezekiel is asked to 'prophesy to these bones' and to command them 'to hear the word of the Lord'. To declare God's word is an important stage and in many of our churches this has been faithfully done. But something more is needed. By that word shattered skeletons become individual corpses but they are still lifeless. Preaching the word without the power of God's Spirit entering into the lives of those who hear will only bring a limited restoration. So often what has happened in the Church is that some preachers with prophetic zeal have recognized the deadness of the Church. They have seen dry bones and spoken the Word of God to them but those bones have still remained just as dead. It really is easy for a preacher to go on and on speaking about the deadness of the Church and condemning the lifelessness of a congregation but something more is needed. As my friend Tom Smail says: 'Exhortation is not much use in a graveyard.' When the dead bones receive the Word of the Lord they need to know that there is power to bring them to life. That is why the second stage in Ezekiel's vision is so important. He is asked 'to prophesy to the wind (the word is breath or spirit), and appeal to that spirit to come and breathe upon these slain that they may live'. This time the corpses come alive and stand on their feet. As John B. Taylor comments on this passage: 'This time the effect was devastating. What preaching by itself failed to achieve prayer made a reality.'[5]

I believe the word that God is speaking to us particularly in the Irish Churches today is a word of judgement but also a word of mercy and of hope. A word of judgement for all our pride and hardness of heart, for the way in which we have had a 'form of godliness but denied its power'. He is challenging us to hear His word of renewal and restoration in a really radical way. It is a word that is spoken by His Spirit when we ourselves are prepared to lay aside our pre-conceived ideas of how He will work and when we pray 'breathe on these slain that they may live'. As Bishop John Taylor so aptly puts it:

> But the Spirit does not give himself where our encounters are glib, masked exchanges of second-hand thoughts. Our defences must be down, broken either by intense joy or by despair. One way or the other we must have come to the end of ourselves. So this shameful humiliation

of Christians, not only in our generation but at all times, is better far than their self-congratulation, for it is pre-requisite of a renewal of the Holy Spirit. It is worth remembering that the root of the words humiliation and humility is humus. To be down in the straw and the dung and the refuse—Paul's words—is to become the soil in which the seed of Christ's manhood falls and dies and brings forth the harvest.

Here is the meeting of the four elements: we, the earth, and the Spirit of the wind, the water and the fire.'[6]

[1] Article by Charles Davis in *America* January 29, 1966.

[2] From *Atheism Irish Style* by Michael Paul Gallagher in the Furrow.

[3] *Unless the Lord build the house.* Page 11. Ralph Martin. Ave Maria Press 1971.

[4] *Christ is alive* Michael Quoist. Page 115. Gill and Macmillan Ltd. 1971.

[5] *Ezekiel—An introduction and commentary* by John B. Taylor, Tyndale Press 1969.

[6] *The Go-Between God,* John V. Taylor. Page 128. S.C.M. Press 1972.

[7] Mrs. B. P. Head 1951.

For Your Meditation

Behold, I send my messenger to prepare the way before me, and the Lord whom you seek will suddenly come to his temple; the messenger of the covenant in whom you delight, behold, he is coming, says the Lord of hosts. But who can endure the day of his coming, and who can stand when he appears ? For he is like a refiner's fire and like fullers' soap; he will sit as a refiner and purifier of silver, and he will purify the sons of Levi and refine them like gold and silver, till they present right offerings to the Lord. Then the offering of Judah and Jerusalem will be pleasing to the Lord as in the days of old and as in former years. Then I will draw near to you for judgement; I will be a swift witness against the sorcerers, against the adulterers, against those who swear falsely, against those who oppress the hireling in his wages, the widow and the orphan, against those who thrust aside the sojourner, and do not fear me, says the Lord of hosts.

For I the Lord do not change; therefore you, O sons of Jacob, are not consumed. From the days of your fathers you have turned aside from my statutes and have not kept them. Return to me, and I will return to you, says the Lord of hosts. But you say, 'How shall we return ?' Will man rob God ? Yet you are robbing me. But you say, 'How are we robbing thee ?' In your tithes and offerings. You are cursed with a curse, for you are robbing me; the whole nation of you. Bring the full tithes into the storehouse, that there may be food in my house; and thereby put to the test, says the Lord of hosts, if I will not open the windows of heaven for you and pour down for you an overflowing blessing. I will rebuke the devourer for you, so that it will not destroy the fruits of your soil; and your vine in the field shall not fail to bear, says the Lord of hosts. Then all nations will call you blessed, for you will be a land of delight, says the Lord of hosts. Your words have been stout against me, says the Lord. Yet you say, 'How have we spoken against thee ?' You have said, 'It is vain to serve God. What is the good of our keeping his charge or of walking as in mourning before the Lord of hosts ? Henceforth we deem the arrogant blessed; evildoers not only prosper but when they put God to the test they escape.' Then those who feared the Lord spoke with one another; the Lord heeded and heard them, and a book of remembrance was written before him of those who feared the Lord and thought on his name. They shall be mine, says the Lord of hosts, my special possession on the day when I act, and I will spare them as a man spares his son who serves him. Then once more you shall distinguish between the righteous and the wicked, between one who serves God and one who does not serve him.

Malachi chapter 3

A Prayer

O Breath of Life, come sweeping through us,
Revive thy Church with life and power,
O Breath of Life, come, cleanse, renew us,
And fit thy Church to meet this hour.

O Wind of God, come bend us, break us,
Till humbly we confess our need:
Then in thy tenderness re-make us,
Revive, restore; for this we plead.

O Breath of Love, come breathe within us,
Renewing thought and will and heart;
Come, love of Christ, afresh to win us,
Revive thy Church in every part.

Revive us, Lord! Is zeal abating
While harvest fields are vast and white?
Revive us, Lord, the world is waiting,
Equip thy Church to spread the light.[7]

2. "Greater Things Than . . ."

> Truly, truly, I say to you, he who believes in me will also do the works that I do; and greater works than these will he do, because I go to the Father.
>
> Saint John 14 v. 12

I wonder how often we have read those familiar words and passed on with utter incredulity, unable to take in the fantastic promise which our Lord was making there. I had often read those words and for some reason had never stopped to think of their implication for today. Over the past few years I have often read those important chapters 14, 15, 16 and 17 of the Gospel according to St. John. They are breath-taking in the challenge which they set before us. They were not just words to fill up time in an after dinner speech nor pleasantries to comfort the fearful disciples. They were the powerfully inspired words of the Son of God to teach disciples of every age what to expect when they follow Christ. They were the marching orders for the infant Church about to be born and they are re-issued to the Church in every age.

Time and time again in the course of His final address to the disciples the Lord promised the power of His Holy Spirit to come within them. As He spoke about leaving them and returning to the Father He sensed their anxiety and fear. 'Where I am going you cannot come now,' He said.

> Let not your hearts be troubled; believe in God believe also in me. In my Father's house are many rooms; if it were not so, would I have told you that I go to prepare a place for you, I will come again and will take you to myself, that where I am you may be also.
>
> Saint John 14 vs. 1-3

While He was with them in His physical body He was confined to place and time. Now He explained that in His risen power He would be with each disciple for ever. He would come by the power of His Spirit to live in each one of them.

> But the Counsellor, the Holy Spirit, whom the Father will send in my name, he will teach you all things, and bring to your remembrance all that I have said to you.
>
> Saint John 14 v. 26

> Nevertheless I tell you the truth: it is to your advantage that I go away, for if I do not go away, the Counsellor will not come to you; but if I go, I will send him to you. And when he comes, he will convince the world concerning sin and righteousness and judgement: concerning sin, because they do not believe in me; concerning righteousness because I go to the Father, and you will see me no more; concerning judgement, because the ruler of this world is judged. I have yet many things to say to you, but you cannot bear them now. When the Spirit of truth comes, he will guide you into all the truth; for he will not speak on his own authority, but whatever he hears he will speak, and he will declare to you the things that are to come. He

will glorify me, for he will take what is mine and declare it to you. All that the Father has is mine; therefore I said that he will take what is mine and declare it to you.

Saint John 16 vs. 7-15

Not surprisingly the disciples found His teaching hard to take. How incredible it must have sounded to them! How impossible! They had seen Christ raise the dead and heal the sick. They had been with Him when blind eyes were opened and deaf ears stopped. Lepers were healed by His touch of love and men and women whose lives had had no meaning or purpose were suddenly flooded with new vitality. Now He was saying quite calmly and confidently to them, ordinary human beings: I am going to so come and live within you that in my name and through the power of my indwelling spirit you will be able to do the works that I have done and even greater works you will do.

The fact is they proved it true. When we turn the pages of the New Testament to the Acts of the Apostles we find that promise gloriously fulfilled on almost every page. As Christ had promised, His Holy Spirit came in power upon those men and women on the Day of Pentecost and endued them with the strength to do what He had said they would do. The seemingly impossible had happened. Frightened, self-conscious, inhibited, ordinary men and women were transformed into living witnesses to the power of God. With one mind and one voice they gave glory to God and demonstrated His power to work the same miracles that Christ had done during His earthly life. Men and women's bodies and minds were healed, intractable enemies of the Christian way became convinced Christians, three thousand on the day of Pentecost alone. Prison doors were opened, prayer was answered. As one contemporary observer noted: They turned the world upside down.

When I was a student in theological college I had often read those stories in the Acts of the Apostles and with great wistfulness I had often asked myself: What has happened to that Church ? Was that power only for the first century? Was it only a demonstration of the 'first fine careless rapture' of the infant Church, or could it be for today ? By many I was led to believe it was only for their day.

I was told that such demonstrations of power were necessary in the early days to convince a pagan society. They were no longer necessary or to be expected since we had all the institutions of Christianity and the written words of Scripture. I have come to see how pathetically sad, such a position is. What a travesty it is of our Lord's promise. 'You shall receive power when the Holy Spirit is come upon you and you shall be my witnesses.' There is more than a little truth in Bishop John Taylor's words : 'All these drab infidelities are committed not because too little power is available to us, but because the power so far exceeds the petty scale we want to live by. He has made us little lower than gods, while our highest ambition is to be a little above the Joneses. We are looking for a 'family-size God, dispensing pep-pills and tranquilizers as required with a Holy Spirit who is a baby's comforter; no wonder the Lord of terrible aspect is too much for us ! '[1]

I remember as a student reading for the first time with great joy and excitement J. B. Phillips' translation of the Acts of the Apostles and the Epistles of St. Paul. Something which he wrote in his introduction to those translations struck me with great force and remained with me as a constant challenge in the early days of my ministry.

It is impossible to spend several months in close study of the remarkable short book, convention-

34

ally known as the Acts of the Apostles, without being profoundly stirred and, to be honest, disturbed. The reader is stirred because he is seeing Christianity, the real thing, in action for the first time in human history. The new-born Church, as vulnerable as any human child, having neither money nor influence nor power in the ordinary sense, is setting forth joyfully and courageously to win the pagan world for God through Christ. The young Church, like all young creatures, is appealing in its simplicity and single-heartedness. Here we are seeing the Church in its first youth, valiant and unspoiled—a body of ordinary men and women joined in an unconquerable fellowship never before seen on this earth.

Yet we cannot help feeling disturbed as well as moved, for this surely is the Church as it was meant to be. It is vigorous and flexible, for these are the days before it ever became fat and short of breath through prosperity, or muscle-bound by over-organisation. These men did not make 'acts of faith', they believed; they did not 'say their prayers', they really prayed. They did not hold conferences on psychosomatic medicine, they simply healed the sick. But if they were uncomplicated and naive by modern standards we have ruefully to admit that they were open on the God-ward side in a way that is almost unknown today.

No one can read this book without being convinced that there is Someone here at work besides mere human beings. Perhaps because of their very simplicity, perhaps because of their readiness to believe, to obey, to give, to suffer, and if need be to die, the Spirit of God found what surely He must always be seeking—a fellowship of men and women so united in love and faith that He can work in them and through them with the minimum of let or hindrance. Consequently it is a matter of sober historical fact that never before has any small body of ordinary people so moved the world that their enemies could say, with tears of rage in their eyes, that these men 'have turned the world upside down !' (17 v. 6)[2]

In his preface to his translation of *The Letters to the Young Churches* he observed that as he spent years in close study of those letters their vitality came over so vividly that he sometimes felt as if he were an electrician rewiring an ancient house without being able to turn the mains off. Later J. B. Phillips observed :

> When we compare the strength and vigour of the Spirit-filled early Church with the confused and sometimes feeble performance of the Church today, we might perhaps conclude that when man's rigidity attempts to canalise the free and flexible flow of the Spirit he is left to his own devices.

Thank God that in this hour of almost universal darkness God's power is being renewed. It is when we become 'open on the God-ward side' and realise 'it is not by might nor by power but by God's Spirit' we are able to release His power to work again. What I see now is what I had longed to see. Not just a return to that first century which is impossible except in nostalgic phantasy, but a real renewal of God's power in the world through the Church today. His promise is being fulfilled in our day that we who believe in Him will do the works that He has done and even greater works shall we do. What I have come to see is that the Acts of the Apostles did not end

36

with Chapter 28. Thousands of chapters have been written since then. I don't know what chapter we are in today but it is an exciting one that the Holy Spirit is writing in the world of the 70's. It almost seems that out of the dark tunnel of the sixties with all the blind alleys that we followed, God is speaking a new word to His people. It is a word of resurrection in the face of death, decay and destruction. It is a word of light and comfort and of love in a dark, dismal and despairing world. It is a word of power for a helpless world that has lost its way. The breath of God's Spirit is blowing through the dry bones of our institutional churches and bringing new vitality. It is impossible to keep abreast of the Spirit's moving in the hearts and lives of men and women all over the world. Daily news comes in of a new outpouring of God's Spirit in the lives of individuals and groups of people.

The features of this renewal are:

A new awareness of God

Men and women are realising that 'God is not dead'. He is very much alive and active in the world to radically change lives and situations. We are seeing again that God is only limited by our unbelief and disobedience; that when our lives are open to His mighty power great things are happening 'far beyond all that we ask or think'.

A new devotion to Jesus Christ as Lord

Before His death our Lord promised: 'I, if I be lifted up from the earth will draw all men unto me.' As the Church uplifts Jesus as Lord, men and women whose hearts are hungry for reality are being brought into a new and living relationship with Christ. The Church is inspired with a new confidence to 'lift Jesus higher' throughout the world that all men might acknowledge and worship God's 'last word to mankind'. 'For we do not yet see all things put under Him but we see Jesus, made lower than the angels, now crowned with honour and glory.'

A renewal of the gifts of the Holy Spirit

The 'Charismata' or grace gifts of the Spirit of God which have never been absent from the Church are being shown again to upbuild the Church in love and to make it a powerful instrument in witness to an unbelieving world. The charismatic gifts are not the exclusive possession of an élitist group of super Christians neither are they toys for immature people. They are the very tools of God offered to His people, to edify His Church and demonstrate His power in the world. One of the urgent needs of the Church today is a thorough understanding of the operation of the gifts of the Spirit as outlined in the New Testament and particularly in such passages as I Corinthians chapters 12, 13 and 14. St. Paul's prayer for the Christians at Corinth is surely God's wish for the Church in every generation.

> So that you are not lacking in any spiritual gift, as you wait for the revealing of our Lord Jesus Christ.
>
> 1 Corinthians 1 v. 7

An identity as the children of God

I remember as a boy being rather puzzled and amused by the first question in the catechism in the Church of Ireland Book of Common Prayer. It simply was: 'What is your name?' In response you said your Christian name or names! I have now come to see how important that question really is. So many of us as Christians do not really know 'who we are'. We have not discovered our new name as sons of the living God, 'heirs of God and joint heirs with Christ'. Through the renewing and indwelling power of God's Spirit men and women are becoming aware of their identity.

> For all who are led by the Spirit of God are
> sons of God. For you did not receive the spirit
> of slavery to fall back into fear, but you have
> received the spirit of sonship. When we cry,
> 'Abba! Father!' it is the Spirit himself bearing
> witness with our spirit that we are children of
> God, and if children, then heirs, heirs of God
> and fellow heirs with Christ, provided we suffer
> with him in order that we may also be glorified
> with him.

> Romans 8 vs. 14-17

A new love for scripture as the Word of God

God's word is becoming for many in a new way a
'lamp to their feet and a light to their path'. I have seen
the Bible come alive as a 'word for today' to so many
people who are prepared to allow the Spirit to lead them
in their understanding.

A new urgency in evangelism

Every Christian was an evangelist in the early Church
and the Holy Spirit is renewing that conviction again
today. The Holy Spirit is giving to quite ordinary men
and women a new power to speak without fear about
Jesus Christ and what He means to them. In the Epilogue
to his fascinating book *Evangelism in the Early Church*
Michael Green drew attention to a feature of first century
Christianity which is being renewed today in many
refreshing ways. He observed:

> Their love, their joy, their changed habits and
> progressively transformed characters gave great
> weight to what they had to say. Their community
> life, though far from perfect, as Christian writers
> were constantly complaining, was nevertheless

39

sufficiently different and impressive to attract notice, to invite curiosity, and to inspire discipleship in an age that was as pleasure-conscious. as materialistic and as devoid of serious purpose as our own. Paganism saw in early Christianity a quality of living, and supremely of dying, which could not be found elsewhere.

Unless there is a transformation of contemporary church life so that once again the task of evangelism is something which is seen as incumbent on every baptized Christian, and is backed up by a quality of living which outshines the best that unbelief can muster, we are unlikely to make much headway through techniques of evangelism. Men will not believe that Christians have good news to share until they find that bishops and bakers, university professors and housewives, bus drivers and street corner preachers are all alike keen to pass it on, however different their methods may be. And men will continue to believe that the Church is an introverted society composed of 'respectable' people and bent on its own preservation until they see in Church groupings and individual Christians the caring, the joy, the fellowship, the self-sacrifice and the openness which marked the early Church at its best.[3]

A new understanding of 'the body of Christ'

The Holy Spirit is bringing to life in the experience of thousands of people something which for a long time they had only known as a rather pleasant theological or liturgical phrase. After the outpouring of the Holy Spirit at Pentecost St. Luke records that the early Christians were drawn together in a deep commitment to one another in 'community living'. In a wide variety of ways this sense of our togetherness in the body of Christ is being renewed as Christians are coming together often from very varied backgrounds and traditions to express through their life of worship and witness something of the meaning of the body of Christ on earth. Religious communities which had become simply 'dormitories' for individuals 'doing their own thing' have become communities of mutual concern and fellowship. Parishes and churches which were fragmented and coldly formal have become alive with warmth and welcome. Fellowships which had become introverted and exclusive have opened out in real caring service to meet the needs of others. Homes have become extended families where lonely and needy people are welcomed in Christ's name and given a status and a dignity which they had lost in an impersonal society. I know one home in Dublin which is typical of quite a few. The young couple have just bought a small three-bedroomed house which they and their three children are joyfully sharing with others. The last time I visited their home all the furniture in their living room consisted of a carpet and four chairs. Regularly up to forty or fifty people will crowd into that small room and seated on the floor will engage in prayer and Bible Study and fellowship together. Quite ordinary members of the body of Christ are re-discovering the gifts which God is bestowing on them to share with those in need.

Writing recently about his experience of God's power to work deeply in people's lives through the ministry of others Dr. Frank Lake, an eminent Christian psychiatrist, has written :

> Now we are able to say quite confidently, that where the Holy Spirit is present in power within the Body of Christ, in a loving, praying group of Christians, people are enabled by the exercise of the ministry gifts, to reach down to and

re-own the painful memories of earliest infancy and childhood. They relive these experiences, cared for by the surrounding group, in such a way as to be free from bondage to the powerful figures of the past, to outworn inhibitions, and to the very roots of those character patterns which were established in order to cope with overwhelming situations.

In the 'deliverance ministries' now manifesting themselves by the love and power of our Heavenly Father, in charismatic prayer groups, whether they be Roman Catholic, Anglican, Free Church, Pentecostal, or, as so often nowadays, mixed, the power of Christ released by the Holy Spirit is effecting the redemption of man in these primary depths of his nature.

This is new wine. It needs new bottles. The great lesson of our day is that 'new bottles' does not mean new denominations. It means new ways of inter-personal relating, new structures, no doubt, for small group meetings alongside the ongoing life of parochial institutions. The small group members, from the intensified cycle of their relationships with the Spirit and each other, infuse the congregational life with a new loving and caring intimacy. The whole remains rooted and grounded in the worship, Word, Sacrament and Fellowship which have been our heritage all along.[4]

A new awareness of worship

He has put a new song in my mouth; a song of praise to our God, many will see it and fear and put their trust in the Lord.

Psalm 40 v. 3

One of the most distinctive marks of the early Church was the joy expressed in the lives of its members. St. Luke records in Acts chapter 2:

> And day by day, attending the temple together and breaking bread in their homes, they partook of food with glad and generous hearts, praising God and having favour with all the people. And the Lord added to their number day by day those who were being saved.
>
> Acts 2 vs. 46 & 47

When the Holy Spirit came upon the early disciples they were so filled with joy that they appeared to the on-lookers to be drunk! What a contrast with most of our congregations today. It's hardly the first conclusion a bystander would reach on seeing the average congregation emerging from Sunday worship. Yet in the very first sermon preached by Peter he had to begin by explaining that he and his companions were not drunk.

> But Peter, standing with the eleven, lifted up his voice and addressed them, Men of Judea and all who dwell in Jerusalem, let this be known to you, and give ear to my words. For these men are not drunk, as you suppose, since it is only the third hour of the day; but this is what was spoken by the prophet Joel: And in the last days it shall be, God declares, that I will pour out my Spirit upon all flesh, and your sons and your daughters shall prophesy and your young men shall see visions, and your old men shall dream dreams; yea, and on my menservants and my maidservants in those days I will pour out my Spirit.
>
> Acts 2 vs. 14-18a

Ever since with every fresh outpouring of God's Spirit on the Church there has been a new upsurge of joy

43

expressing itself in worship and praise. Out of a fresh new awareness of the reality of God, of His faithfulness, love and mercy springs a real joy that is hard to contain. When we see God acting and moving in power, we want to praise and thank Him. Indeed the word 'worship' is derived from an old English word 'WORTHSHIP' which simply means we want to tell God what He is worth to us. He is worth loving. He is worth thanking. He is worth giving everything to. This was the experience of so many of those who wrote the Psalms of the Old Testament. In countless songs of praise they extolled the majesty and might, the power and glory of God.

> O come, let us sing to the Lord; let us make a joyful noise to the rock of our salvation ! Let us come into his presence with thanksgiving; let us make a joyful noise to him with songs of praise ! For the Lord is a great God, and a great King above all gods. In his hand are the depths of the earth; the heights of the mountains are his also. The sea is his, for he made it; for his hands formed the dry land. O come, let us worship and bow down, let us kneel before the Lord, our Maker ! For he is our God, and we are the people of his pasture, and the sheep of his hand. O that today you would hearken to his voice !

> Psalm 95 vs. 1-7

God is restoring that sense of praise to His people. We are finding that the ancient psalms and songs and canticles are becoming vibrant with life and meaning when the Holy Spirit touches our lives with renewing power. The famous opening words of the shorter catechism of the Presbyterian Church are a constant challenge to the deadness of so much Church worship. 'Man's chief end is to glorify God and to enjoy Him for ever.' Worship ought to be the most joyful expression of

44

our lives. Yet I have often looked down on a congregation of people with long faces singing some of Wesley's great hymn :

> O for a thousand tongues to sing
> My dear Redeemer's praise.

Evelyn Underhill was surely being prophetic when she wrote to Church of England clergy in 1928 :

> We are drifting towards a religion which consciously or unconsciously, keeps its eye on humanity rather than on deity—a religion which lays all the stress on service and hardly any on awe.

When we stand in awe of God and really praise Him for who He is and what He has done we begin to see Him working in a new way in our lives and in the world. To truly praise God is perhaps the most revolutionary thing that the Church is called to do. It changes things. Notice what happened to the Virgin Mary when she began to praise God for what He had already done but also for what He was going to do ! In the Magnificat she proclaimed a spiritual, social and economic revolution that turns all political and human systems on end. When God's people truly praise Him the glory of God is revealed. Glory is the visible expression of the power and presence of God with His people and when we praise so much that God's glory is unfolded then all who come near cannot fail to be moved. One of the most remarkable examples of this in the Old Testament is the account in 2 Chronicles chapter 5 of the dedication of the great Temple at Jerusalem in the reign of King Solomon. Solomon had assembled all the great orchestra and choir in the Temple to plan and sing in a unison of praise to God in the words:

> For He is good,
> for His steadfast love endures forever.

45

The result of that unison of praise was dramatic and real.

> The house, the house of the Lord was filled with a cloud, so that the priests could not stand to minister because of the cloud; for the glory of the Lord filled the house of God.

I believe that was not to be a unique experience. God meant it to be a living and constant experience for His people when they came together to acknowledge His power, His love and His majesty. The problem in so many of our Churches is that we have so often concentrated on 'singing' and we have never learned what it means to 'praise' God. So often in our Churches we have excellent singing by well-trained choirs accompanied by impeccable playing of the organ. It would stand well alongside any concert performance. But God does not want His people to perform He wants us to praise.

> Sing to God, sing praises to his name.
>
> Psalm 68 v. 4

Praise comes from the heart and can be expressed in a variety of ways including singing. The Psalms and the Old Testament speak of many means of praising God. There are eight separate Hebrew words in the Old Testament translated 'sing' in the Authorised Version of the Bible. One of the words means 'to shout or sing aloud for joy'. Another, 'a shout of gladness and rejoicing' and another 'a joyful voice singing and triumphing'.

Over the past two years I have had the joy of working closely with a choir of 80 young people in Northern Ireland. Drawn from a wide variety of Church traditions, they were assembled to share the musical *Come Together in Jesus Name*. This is an experience in Christian love and joyful worship that has had a profound effect on countless thousands of people of all ages in many parts of the world.

46

'Come Together' represents a real attempt to encourage participation in worship and praise so that people might be led into a deeper awareness of God and of all He has done for them. The Choir has been invited to share 'Come Together' all over Ireland and in the two years when we have been together upwards on 20,000 people have participated from all walks of life and all religious backgrounds. I have never worked with such a dedicated group of young people. In our experience together we have begun to learn what it means to praise as well as to sing. Every week those young people came together; there were students, nurses, shop assistants, doctors. For over two hours they rehearsed not only by practising the music but in prayer for one another. The result was amazing when we came before an audience. We were as one. I remember the evening when we led the programme in the Mansion House in Dublin; we had spent over half an hour in prayer before going out to the platform. The prayer turned to praise before we left the room where we were and the glory of God came down upon the place that night. Time and time again we have known people who have been led into a personal encounter with Christ as we have shared in His praise and eternity alone will reveal all who found the Saviour through the songs of 'Come Together'. There is power in praise. I remember hearing after another performance in Dublin about a young Jewish boy who had accompanied a friend. He got up half way through and said to his friend: 'I'll have to go or I'm in danger of losing my faith!' The lessons we have learned together we want to share with our local Churches so that we all might be able to enter in to His courts with praise and really enjoy God.

One of the great fallacies which we have fallen into is that we should only praise God when we feel good. The Bible speaks of a 'sacrifice of praise', and we learn that with St. Paul we can praise God in every situation. We

47

can have the 'mantle of praise instead of a faint spirit' (Isaiah 61 v. 3). Time and time again that spirit is expressed in the Old Testament but perhaps nowhere more nobly than by the prophet Habakkuk. He lived six hundred years before Christ and he foresaw the impending doom that was coming to his country.

> O Lord, how long shall I cry for help, and thou wilt not hear ? or cry to thee 'Violence !' and thou wilt not save ? Why dost thou make me see wrongs and look upon trouble ? Destruction and violence are before me; strife and contention arise. So the law is slacked and justice never goes forth. For the wicked surround the righteous, so justice goes forth perverted.
>
> Habakkuk 1 vs. 1-4

In the midst of impending destruction and foreboding doom he was able to praise God.

> Though the fig tree do not blossom, no fruit be on the vines, the produce of the olive fail and the fields yield no food, the flock be cut off from the fold and there be no herd in the stalls, yet I will rejoice in the Lord, I will joy in the God of my salvation. God, the Lord, is my strength; he makes my feet like hinds' feet, he makes me tread upon my high places.
>
> Habakkuk 3 vs. 17-19

In the Acts of the Apostles St. Luke records the terrible treatment which Paul and Silas received first at the hands of the mob who attacked them and then at the hands of the magistrates who tore the clothes off their backs and had them beaten with rods. Bruised and bleeding with multiple injuries they were thrown into the stinking, dark inner prison, their feet fastened to the stocks. In the midst of all their terrible suffering at midnight they were praying and praising God when suddenly there was a mighty miracle—the prison doors were opened by the force of an earthquake and everyone's fetters were unfastened. Their great release led to the conversion of the jailer and his family. What power there is in praise even when we don't feel like it !

> I will bless the Lord at all times; his praise shall continually be in my mouth. My soul makes its boast in the Lord; let the afflicted hear and be glad. O magnify the Lord with me, and let us exalt his name together ! I sought the Lord, and he answered me, and delivered me from all my fears. Look to him, and be radiant; so your faces shall never be ashamed. This poor man cried, and the Lord heard him, and saved him out of all his troubles.
>
> Psalm 34 vs. 1-6

St. John the Divine in the deprivation and suffering which he experienced in the salt mines of Patmos found himself transported in praise with the angels and archangels.

> Worthy art thou, our Lord and God, to receive glory and honour and power, for thou didst create all things, and by thy will they existed and were created.
>
> Revelation 4 v. 11

In the praise of the people of God we are called to share in the joy and praise of heaven, in the communion of the saints to sing the 'song of Moses and the Lamb'.

> Great and wonderful are thy deeds, O Lord God the Almighty ! Just and true are thy ways, O King of the ages ! Who shall not fear and glorify thy name, O Lord ? For thou alone art holy. All nations shall come and worship thee, for thy judgements have been revealed.
>
> Revelation 15 vs. 3 & 4

Heaven comes down and glory fills our souls when with the great multitude like the sound of mighty waters and like the sound of mighty thunderpeals we cry:

> Hallelujah! For the Lord our God the Almighty reigns. Let us rejoice and exult and give Him the glory.
>
> Revelation 19 vs. 6 & 7

This rejoicing and exultation finds expression not only in the singing of the praise of God's people but also in many bodily expressions of praise. Because we have limited praise to singing in our Churches for so long we have neglected so many other expressions of praise which are equally valid when they convey the praise of the heart. The Psalmist encourages people to clap their hands and shout in praise.

> Clap your hands, all peoples! Shout to God with loud songs of joy!
>
> Psalm 47 v. 1

Again we are encouraged by the example of the Psalmist to lift our hands up in praise to God.

> So I will bless thee as long as I live; I will lift up my hands and call on thy name.
>
> Psalm 63 v. 4

> Lift up your hands to the holy place, and bless the Lord!
>
> Psalm 134 v. 2

I have been present in congregations of eight or ten people and in congregations of eight or ten thousand when together we have been able to leave down our hymn books and lift our hands in praise to God, Father, Son and Holy Spirit.

Another expression of praise to God is the dance. 'Praise Him with the timbrel and dance' says the Psalmist in Psalm 150 and he goes on to mention many other

50

instruments that we can use in praise to God.

How strange it is that in so many Churches we have consecrated the organ as the only fit instrument for God's praise! And how unscriptural too! It often amuses me when people object to a guitar accompaniment in Church. The Psalmist certainly would have raised no objection to the guitar and drums so long as they were used in the praise of God.

> Praise Him with strings and pipe! Praise Him with sounding cymbals; praise Him with loud clashing cymbals! Let everything that breathes praise the Lord! Praise the Lord!
>
> Psalm 150 vs. 4-6

There is the praise in tongues as the Spirit inspires new songs in the people of God. It is so moving to be present with others when the Spirit leads a congregation out in praise and worship in tongues which He inspires. It is 'the music of heaven' and is meant to be in the experience of any congregation as they praise God. It cannot be rehearsed or worked up. It comes like the dew in the evening and refreshes us as we enter the courts of heaven.

There is the praise of silence which often follows 'singing in tongues'. As we enter into the holy of holies and adore and worship the Lord in the new song He inspires we are led to the silence of awe and reverent devotion.

What a wonderful variety there is in the praise which God inspires and we are only beginning to experience it again in the Church. It is the breath of the Spirit of God that brings reality into our worship. For so long in the Church what we thought we had to do was to make worship relevant, change the language, brush up the tunes, sing the old hymns to modern tunes. Relevance is important but it is the *reality* of our worship that will convince

51

the world that we mean what we say. Then when 'an unbeliever or outsider enters ... falling on his face he will worship God and declare that God is really among you'. (1 Corinthians 14 vs. 24, 25).

(1) *The Go-between God,* John V. Taylor.

(2) *The Young Church in Action.* Page 11. J. B. Phillips. *Fontana Books* 1959.

(3) *Evangelism in the Early Church* by Michael Green. Page 274 *Hodder and Stoughton* 1970.

(4) *Listening and Responding* by Dr. Frank Lake. Page 10. A publication by *The Clinical Theology Association*, Nottingham.

For Your Meditation

Ho, every one who thirsts, come to the waters; and he who has no money, come, buy and eat ! Come, buy wine and milk without money and without price. Why do you spend your money for that which is not bread, and your labour for that which does not satisfy ? Hearken diligently to me, and eat what is good, and delight yourselves in fatness. Incline your ear, and come to me; hear, that your soul may live; and I will make with you an everlasting covenant, my steadfast, sure love for David. Behold, I made him a witness to the peoples, a leader and commander for the peoples. Behold, you shall call nations that you know not, and nations that knew you not shall run to you, because of the Lord your God, and of the Holy One of Israel, for he has glorified you. Seek the Lord while he may be found, call upon him while he is near; let the wicked forsake his way, and the unrighteous man his thoughts; let him return to the Lord, that he may have mercy on him, and to our God, for he will abundantly pardon. For my thoughts are not your thoughts, neither are your ways my ways, says the Lord. For as the heavens are higher than the earth, so are my ways higher than your ways and my thoughts than your thoughts. For as the rain and the snow come down from heaven, and return not thither but water the earth, making it bring forth and sprout, giving seed to the sower and bread to the eater, so shall my word be that goes forth from my mouth; it shall not return to me empty, but it shall accomplish that which I purpose, and prosper in the thing for which I sent it. For you shall go out in joy, and be led forth in peace; the mountains and the hills before you shall break forth into singing, and all the trees of the field shall clap their hands. Instead of the thorn shall come up the cypress; instead of the brier shall come up the myrtle; and it shall be to the Lord for a memorial, for an everlasting sign which shall not be cut off.

Isaiah chapter 55

A Prayer

Lord God and Father, in the death and resurrection of Jesus Christ your Son you willed to reconcile all mankind to yourself and to reconcile men with each other in peace. Hear the prayer of your people in this year of grace and salvation. Let your Spirit of life and holiness renew us, in the depths of our being: unite us throughout our life to the risen Christ: for he is our brother and saviour. Father, of your great goodness, hear in the words of your people the prayer of the Spirit to the praise of your glory and the salvation of men. Through Jesus Christ your Son our Lord, the Way, the Truth, and the Life, for ever and ever. Amen.

3. "All Things New"

Reconciliation begins in the heart of God. He longs that all that He has created might be restored to the harmony that He intended.

In the record of the Old Testament we have a picture of God reaching out to man in every possible way to break down the barriers which man has created. In mercy and appealing love He revealed Himself to erring Israel. Through His servants, the prophets, God repeatedly spoke to His people calling them to faith and fellowship with Himself. The lovely words of the prophet Hosea are typical of the many ways in which this plea is expressed.

> When Israel was a child, I loved him, and out of Egypt I called my son. The more I called them, the more they went from me; they kept sacrificing to the Baals, and burning incense to idols. Yet it was I who taught Ephraim to walk, I took them up in my arms; but they did not know that I healed them. I led them with cords of compassion, with the bands of love, and I became to them as one who eases the yoke on their jaws, and I bent down to them and fed them.
>
> Hosea 11 vs. 1-4

A similar plea comes through the prophet Isaiah:
Come now, let us reason together, says the Lord:

though your sins are like scarlet, they shall be as white as snow; though they are red like crimson, they shall become like wool.

Isaiah 1 v. 18

When His people would not listen God sent His own Son to be born of a woman, silently to enter the world He loved and share the lot of man.

In many and various ways God spoke of old to our fathers by the prophets; but in these last days He has spoken to us by a Son.

Hebrews 1 vs. 1 & 2

He came to where we are to bring us to where He is.

In parable after parable Jesus tried to illustrate the Father's heart of love. He is like the Waiting Father who day after day awaits the return of the Prodigal and when he sees him returning runs to greet him and throws his arms around him. He is the Good Shepherd who fearlessly searches across the dark and wild mountainside and tenderly returns with the lamb on His shoulders.

In accepting the Mission which the Father had called Him to share the Lord deliberately quoted from the prophet Isaiah:

The Spirit of the Lord is upon me, because he has anointed me to preach good news to the poor. He has sent me to proclaim release to the captives and recovering of sight to the blind, to set at liberty those who are oppressed, to proclaim the acceptable year of the Lord.

Saint Luke 4 vs. 18 & 19

Release, recovery and freedom are all the fruits of the reconciling love of God manifest in Jesus Christ.

Beyond His teaching, however, it is perhaps in the Lord's prayer recorded in John 17 that we have the most profound insight into the concern of our Lord for reconciliation.

Having prayed for His disciples He then turned to pray for 'those who believe in me through their word', that is you and me. How incredible it is that the Lord should have had you and me on His heart as He prayed that 'high priestly prayer'. In Hebrews 7: 25 we read that the Lord Jesus 'ever lives to make intercession for us'. Is it too much to believe that it is along those lines that He is praying for us now:

> I do not pray for these only, but also for those who believe in me through their word, that they may all be one; even as thou, Father, art in me, and I in thee, that they also may be in us, so that the world may believe that thou hast sent me. The glory which thou hast given me I have given to them, that they may be one even as we are one, I in them and thou in me, that they may become perfectly one, so that the world may know that thou hast sent me and hast loved them even as thou hast loved me. Father, I desire that they also, whom thou hast given me, may be with me where I am, to behold my glory which thou hast given me in thy love for me before the foundation of the world. O righteous Father, the world has not known thee, but I have known thee; and these know that thou hast sent me. I made known to them thy name, and I will make it known, that the love with which thou hast loved me may be in them, and I in them.

Saint John 17 vs. 20-26

Our Lord here prays quite simply that His people should be a UNITED community, SHARING THE GLORY OF GOD and so BOUND TOGETHER in LOVE that the world will believe in Him through their witness.

In the Bible glory means God's manifestation of Himself in presence and power in the midst of His people. When God's people experience the unity of the Spirit the glory of God is revealed:

> Behold how good and pleasant it is when brothers dwell in unity! It is like the dew of Hermon, which falls on the mountains of Zion. For there the Lord has commanded the blessing, life for evermore.
>
> Psalm 133 vs. 1 & 3

When the Christian Church is united in the power of the risen Christ and reflects the glory of the Father in the love which the Spirit gives then the world will realise that Jesus Christ is Lord. And the amazing truth is that today we can be the answer to the Lord's prayer. As we enter into the reconciliation which Christ has wrought for us on the Cross we become 'agents of His reconciliation'. In a very wonderful way this is what I see God by His Holy Spirit doing in the world.

In every part of the world today God's Spirit is creating in men and women's hearts a hunger and thirst for the reality of the living God. Over the past few years I have had the joy of meeting people from many nations and from every corner of the world one hears the same story of men and women from all backgrounds and traditions coming to a living experience of God's power. In every individual case it is a miracle of a new creation. Some out of the anguish of despair, some through the crucible of doubt—all have come to a real faith in the living Christ. A. W. Tozer, a prophet of our time, has put it very succinctly:

> In this hour of all-but-universal darkness, one cheering gleam appears — within the fold of conservative Christianity there are to be found increasing numbers of persons whose religious

lives are marked by a growing hunger after God himself. They are eager for spiritual realities, and will not be put off with words, nor will they be content with correct interpretations of the truth. They are athirst for God, and will not be satisfied until they have drunk deep at the Fountain of Living Water.[1]

What God is doing by His Spirit in the world today is not just giving a release of joy in individual lives once bound in sin and despair, though thank God it is that. God is moving by His spirit to bring in His new creation —the Kingdom of His Son. He is restoring broken humanity, renewing the face of the earth.

The same Spirit who brooded over the void and darkness and from it brought order in creation is now moving across the world's disorder to bring to birth God's new creation. What God is doing by His Spirit today has global significance and thank God He is restoring that vision to His people.

That was the great desire in the heart of the Son of God when He hung there on the Cross:

> God so loved the world that He gave His only Son, that whoever believes in Him should not perish but have eternal life.

> Saint John 3 v. 16

That was the great vision which Saint Paul shared with the early Christians. This is what he wrote to the first century Christians in Ephesus:

> For He has made known to us in all wisdom and insight the mystery of His will, according to His purpose which He set forth in Christ as a plan for the fullness of time, to unite all things in him, things in heaven and things on earth.

> Ephesians 1 vs. 9 & 10

In the letter to the Colossians after penning the magnificent poem about the 'All sufficient Christ' he declares:

> FOR IN HIM ALL THE FULNESS OF GOD WAS PLEASED TO DWELL, AND THROUGH HIM TO RECONCILE TO HIMSELF ALL THINGS, WHETHER ON EARTH OR IN HEAVEN, MAKING PEACE BY THE BLOOD OF HIS CROSS.
>
> Colossians 1 vs. 19 & 20

The Greek word for reconcile there has the force— 'to fully reconcile'. That is God's eternal purpose so to restore this broken world that it reflects the Divine glory. How magnificently Saint Paul expresses it in the J. B. Phillips translation of Romans 8 vs. 19-21 :

> The whole creation is on tiptoe to see the wonderful sight of the sons of God coming into their own. The world of creation cannot as yet see reality, not because it chooses to be blind, but because in God's purpose it has been so limited—yet it has been given hope. And the hope is that in the end the whole of created life will be rescued from the tyranny of change and decay, and have its share in that magnificent liberty which can only belong to the children of God.

That liberty of the Children of God is being revealed as God's people all over the world are experiencing a new release of the power of God's Holy Spirit just as those early Christians did on the Day of Pentecost. In the world today God is moving by His Spirit 'according to plan'.

This truth has been brought home to me very clearly in two recent International Conferences which I have had the privilege to attend. The first was the 9th International Conference of the Catholic Charismatic Renewal held in

Rome over the 1975 Pentecost week-end, and the other was the third International Conference of the Charismatic Renewal held in Westminster, London that July.

In Rome over 10,000 people from more than 50 nations were together for a Conference under the general theme of 'Renewal and Reconciliation'. The unity and the joy which the Holy Spirit gave is something I shall never forget. I shall long remember the sight of that vast crowd of people from every tongue and nation joining in their praise to Jesus as Lord and Saviour right in the heart of Rome in Saint Peter's Basilica. As that vast congregation reverently sang 'Spirit of the Living God fall afresh on me' and then burst into a joyful 'Singing in tongues' I could not help reflecting that nearly 2000 years ago when the Spirit fell in power on those early Christians there were in the city of Jerusalem 'Strangers from Rome, Jews and Proselytes'. Now there were gathered people from almost every nation finding a real bond of unity in Jesus Christ as Lord and Saviour and singing a new song to the Lamb. As I further reflected on the scene before me I realised how privileged we are in our generation. Saint Peter declared on the Day of Pentecost that Joel's prophecy uttered so long before was now beginning to be fulfilled.

> And in the last days it shall be, God declares, that I will pour out my Spirit upon all flesh, and your sons and your daughters shall prophesy, and your young men shall see visions, and your old men shall dream dreams; yea, and on my menservants and my maidservants in those days I will pour out my Spirit; and they shall prophesy.
>
> Acts 2 vs. 17 & 18

Then it was a vision for those early Christians — a challenge to allow God's Spirit to move in renewing power in the world—we today have the privilege of living in a generation when that vision is becoming more and more a living reality.

In a remarkable way too at that Conference we experienced God's power to reverse the disorder of Babel as the Spirit inspired songs of praise to Jesus Christ as Lord. On the first evening after initial difficulties with translation into four main languages we were sharing in prayer. As we waited in total silence in an atmosphere charged with the presence of God a little bird could be heard singing in the trees beside the arena. I reflected how that bird had no problem with language in offering its praise to God. Just then the quiet hum of singing in the Spirit began to rise from that vast audience till it became a harmonious unison of joyful praise to Father, Son and Holy Spirit.

As we stood there in praise near the tombs of innumerable martyrs who had laid down their lives for Christ we experienced a foretaste of heaven.

> But you have come to Mount Zion and to the city of the living God, the heavenly Jerusalem, and to innumerable angels in festal gathering, and to the assembly of the first-born who are enrolled in heaven, and to a judge who is God of all, and to the spirits of just men made perfect, and to Jesus, the mediator of a new covenant, and to the sprinkled blood that speaks more graciously than the blood of Abel.
>
> Hebrews 12 vs. 22-24

Just as the challenge and vision given to those early Christians demanded the full response of their lives so the Holy Spirit is calling us today to a full commitment to Christ so that the kingdoms of this world might become the Kingdom of our God and His Christ.

That was the challenge that came home again and again to those who attended the Conference in London. God's glory is reflected in His Church, the people of God and He is purifying and purging and cleansing His Church, equipping it with all the gifts and graces of the Spirit to fulfil His mission for the end time. Again there came the stirring challenge which Saint Peter gave long ago to the first-century Christians.

> But you are a chosen race, a royal priesthood, a holy nation God's own people, that you may declare the wonderful deeds of him who called you out of darkness into His marvellous light. Once you were no people but now you are God's people; once you had not received mercy but now you have received mercy.

1 Peter 2 vs. 9 & 10

In the programme 'If my people' which was presented at the Conference we were reminded of the great privilege which we share as the people of God.

> You are the children of the Kingdom of God
> You are the chosen ones for whom the Saviour came.
> You are His noble new creation by the Spirit and the blood
> You are the Church that He has built to bear His name.

But we were also solemnly reminded of the great responsibility which this privilege carries

> You shall be, holy unto me for I the Lord am holy and you shall sanctify yourselves and be holy for I am holy.

God is calling His Church all over the world to a holiness of life, to a renewal in the power of the Holy Spirit so that the world might see a manifestation of the glory of God—'to make plain to all men the meaning of that divine secret which He who created everything has kept hidden from the creation until now. The purpose is that all the angelic powers should now see the complex wisdom of God's plan being worked out through the Church in conformity to that timeless purpose which He centred in Christ Jesus, our Lord' (Ephesians 3 vs. 9-11).

As that 'secret' is being unfolded and men and women are entering into the inheritance of the sons of God it is becoming increasingly clear that if we are to share His glory we will also share His sufferings.

This note so clearly sounded by Saint Paul came through distinctly in prophetic words which were spoken during the final session of the Rome Conference in Saint Peter's Basilica.

> I speak to you of the dawn of a 'new age' for my church. I speak to you of a day that has not been seen before . . . Prepare yourselves for the action that I begin now, because things that you see around you will change; the combat that you must enter now is different; it is new. You need wisdom from me that you do not yet have.
>
> You need the power of my Holy Spirit in a way that you have not possessed it; you need an understanding of my will and of the ways that I work that you do not yet have. Open your eyes, open your hearts to prepare yourselves for me and for the day that I have now begun. My Church will be different; my people will be different; difficulties and trials will come upon you, but the comfort that you will have is the comfort of my Holy Spirit. They will send for you, to take your life, but I will support you. Come to me. Band yourselves together, around me. Prepare, for I proclaim a new day, a day of

victory and of triumph for your God. Behold, it is begun.

Know that I, your God, brought Peter and Paul to Rome to witness to my glory. I have chosen you also and have brought you to Rome to bear witness to my glory, confirmed now by your shepherd. Go forth to the healing of the nations. Know that I am with you; and though you may pass through tribulation and trial, I will be with you even to the end. I am preparing a place for you in glory. Look to me and I will deliver you from the power of the evil one. Behold I am with you now, all days, even till the end of time.

At the beginning of the First National Conference of the Charismatic renewal in Dublin in 1974 God spoke to us of what He is doing in our day with His people

I am lifting you as stones from the dust and building you into my Church.

Out of all our individual and corporate failure of the past God is building a people to His praise, a people who are open to the leading of His Spirit and listening for His direction, a people who are not ashamed to be counted fools for Christ's sake. He showed us further that as He builds His Church we are not to attempt to put the roof on it. For He alone is the Head of the Church.

Come to Him, to that living stone, rejected by men but in God's sight chosen and precious; and like living stones be yourselves built into a spiritual house, to be a holy priesthood, to offer spiritual sacrifices acceptable to God through Jesus Christ.

1 Peter 2 vs. 4 & 5

One of the songs that has become popular in the renewal all over Ireland is the simple one based on

Genesis.

> We are gathering together unto Him
>> Unto Him shall the gathering of the people be
>> We are gathering together unto Him.

As the spokes of a wheel come nearer to each other, as they approach the centre, so God is bringing us together in Him the Centre and heart of the Universe.

> For there is salvation in no one else, for there is no other name under Heaven given among men whereby we must be saved.

Acts 4 v. 12

As the Christian lives in a world rent asunder with so much hatred and division it is with the eye of faith he sees beneath the seething turmoil to the consummation of all things in Christ.

> As it is we do not yet see all things in subjection to him. But we see Jesus crowned with glory and honour.

Hebrews 2 v. 9

[1] *The Pursuit of God* by A. W. Tozer, Christian Publications Inc.

For Your Meditation

He is the image of the invisible God, the first-born of all creation; for in him all things were created in heaven and on earth, visible and invisible, whether thrones or dominions or principalities or authorities — all things were created through him and for him. He is before all things, and in him all things hold together. He is the head of the body, the church; he is the beginning, the first-born from the dead, that in everything he might be pre-eminent. For in him all the fullness of God was pleased to dwell, and through him to reconcile to himself all things, whether on earth or in heaven, making peace by the blood of his cross.

Colossians 1 vs. 15-20

A Prayer

For this reason, because I have heard of your faith in the Lord Jesus and your love toward all the saints I do not cease to give thanks for you, remembering you in my prayers, that the God of our Lord Jesus Christ, the Father of glory, may give you a spirit of wisdom and of revelation in the knowledge of him, having the eyes of your hearts enlightened, that you may know what is the hope to which he has called you, what are the riches of his glorious inheritance in the saints, and what is the immeasurable greatness of his power in us who believe, according to the working of his great might which he accomplished in Christ when he raised him from the dead and made him sit at his right hand in the heavenly places, far above all rule and authority and power and dominion, and above every name that is named, not only in this age but also in that which is to come; and he has put all things under his feet and has made him the head over all things for the church, which is his body, the fullness of him who fills all in all.

Ephesians 1 vs. 15-23

4. "God So Loved"

Reconciliation which begins in the heart of God finds visible expression in the Cross of Christ. With profound simplicity the little children's hymn conveys this truth:

> I sometimes think about the Cross
> And shut my eyes and try to see
> The cruel nails and crown of thorns
> And Jesus crucified for me.
> But even could I see Him die
> I could but see a little part
> Of that great love which like a fire
> Is ever burning in His heart.[1]

In those hours of agony on the Hill of Calvary in a mysterious way 'God was in Christ reconciling the world to Himself'. There 'for our sake God made him to be sin who knew no sin, so that in him we might become the righteousness of God'. Down through the ages theologians and mystics, poets and hymnwriters have tried to express the meaning of this great event, but its full significance defies expression.

Cecil Francis Alexander, the Irish hymnwriter, expressed it very simply:

> We may not know we cannot tell
> What pains He had to bear
> But we believe it was for us
> He hung and suffered there.[2]

Charles Wesley out of the great joy of a personal experience exclaimed:

> And can it be that I should gain
> An interest in the Saviour's blood
> Died He for me, who caused His pain ?
> For me, who Him to death pursued
> Amazing love ! how can it be
> That thou my God, shouldst die for me.
> Tis mystery all ! The immortal dies
> Who can explore His strange design ?
> In vain the firstborn seraph tries
> To sound the depths of love divine !
> Tis mercy all ! let earth adore
> Let angel minds inquire no more.[3]

The basic meaning of reconciliation in the New Testament is well expressed by the simple symbol of the Cross. There is the VERTICAL BAR of the Cross signifying my reconciliation with God and the HORIZONTAL BAR signifying reconciliation between man and man in Christ.

We often use the word reconcile to mean 'making friends'. It is that but in the New Testament its root meaning is the taking away of the barriers to friendship, the complete removal of all that stands in the way, the taking down of the barricades that separate.

When God created man He made him to enjoy fellowship and friendship with Himself. Man by his self will and disobedience built a barrier between himself and God. That friendship was destroyed, the communion broken. Only through what Christ has done by His death and resurrection is it possible for that friendship to be restored and that communion renewed. This is the great truth which Saint Paul expounds in Romans 5 vs. 6-11.

While we were yet helpless, at the right time

71

Christ died for the ungodly. Why, one will hardly die for a righteous man—though perhaps for a good man one will dare even to die. But God shows his love for us in that while we were yet sinners Christ died for us. Since, therefore, we are now justified by his blood, much more shall we be saved by him from the wrath of God. For if while we were enemies we were reconciled to God by the death of his Son, much more, now that we are reconciled, shall we be saved by his life. Not only so, but we also rejoice in God through our Lord Jesus Christ, through whom we have now received our reconciliation.

When Adam disobeyed God he immediately felt a sense of alienation. He felt ashamed and lost. He hid from God among the trees of the garden. Fear gripped him. A barrier which he could not understand nor remove was erected between him and God. Before that Adam had walked with God and talked with God. They had enjoyed sweet communion and fellowship and nothing came between. Now Adam and Eve hid themselves. That beautiful but poignant story in the book of Genesis records in simple outline the story of mankind:

> And they heard the sound of the Lord God walking in the garden in the cool of the day, and the man and his wife hid themselves from the presence of the Lord God among the trees of the garden. But the Lord God called to the man, and said to him, 'Where are you ?'

> Genesis 3 vs. 8 & 9

The story of Adam is the story of every man in his alienation and aloneness. Made for communion with his Maker, made for fellowship with the Divine, man cowers in fear in the corners of the garden of the world God has given us to enjoy. The poets and playwrights of our day are accurately reflecting the true nature of man and it is no accident that the themes of 'lostness' and 'alienation' are so often recurring themes in the plays and poems they write. Man cries out in his despair and his cry echoes back to him with apparent cruel mockery. Colin Wilson, the perceptive author of the book *The Outsider,* declared 'Man is a useless passion, it is meaningless that we live and meaningless that we die.'

But the great truth is that down the corridors of time another voice calls, the voice of the pleading love of God —'Adam, where are you ?', 'John, where are you ?', 'Mary, where are you ?' 'I made you for myself that you might enjoy friendship and fellowship with me. I made you that you might walk freely through the garden of my world; that you might walk with me and talk with me and enjoy sweet communion with me.'

And when Christ died on the Cross we see love's last appeal to sinful and fearful man. In Christ the gap has been bridged—the way—a new and living way made open for man to return to full fellowship with God. All the enmity that stands in the way has been removed and I may return to walk with God and talk with Him. This is the glorious truth of the reconciliation which Christ has won for us on the Cross:

> Therefore, if any one is in Christ, he is a new creation; the old has passed away, behold, the new has come. All this is from God, who through Christ reconciled us to himself and gave us the ministry of reconciliation; that is, God was in Christ reconciling the world to Himself, not counting their trespasses against them, and entrusting to us the message of reconciliation.
>
> 2 Corinthians 5 vs. 17-19

This is the great secret hidden for ages which the Church is called to declare to the world; this is the good news which the world today is longing to hear, the gospel which will set man free from his sin and selfishness, from his fear and his despair.

> There's a way back to God from the dark paths
>   of sin
> At Calvary's cross is where you begin
> When you come as a sinner to Jesus.[4]

When I come to the Cross and kneeling there realise that the God who made me loves me so much then with all my heart I respond to Him in repentance and faith I enter a whole new dimension of living 'the old has passed away the new has come'.

Over the past few years I have met many, young and old who have heard that pleading call of God and turned to find the accepting love of Christ and the beginning of a new creation. I think of many young people who had gone up the blind alley of drugs and alcohol to find some kick and meaning in life and they have come to a real encounter with the living Christ and entered into the real joy of living. What Charles Wesley so powerfully expressed has become their experience.

> No condemnation now I dread
> Jesus, and all in Him is mine
> Alive in Him, my living Head
> And clothed in righteousness Divine.[5]

That is the reality of the new relationship made possible in Christ's reconciling work.

In the week in which I write these words I have had the joy of praying with two people who have come from very different backgrounds to simple faith in Christ. One a brilliant young psychologist who has come out of much anguish of soul and agony of doubt to faith in Christ who cares personally for him and who has opened for him a new dimension of living. The other a dedicated social worker who has tried for years to drown a burden of guilt through escape in alcohol.

For so many of us who have struggled for years to make some meaning out of the tangled web of our lives the very simplicity of Christian faith is puzzling. To be able to realise the amazing grace of God in Christ which accepts us just as we are is so incredible that we find it difficult to accept. We want to earn our salvation. We want to work it out and add our merit. God's Spirit sometimes has to bring us to the end of our tether before we can realise that it is 'not of works lest any man should boast'; 'for by grace are we saved through faith and that not of ourselves, it is the gift of God'. It is a gift which we do nothing to merit or to earn. This was the great truth which Saint Paul had to learn when Christ confronted him on the Damascus road, that all his religious devotion, all his strict adherence to the Jewish law could not save him.

> Though I myself have reason for confidence in the flesh also. If any other man thinks he has reason for confidence in the flesh, I have more: circumcised on the eighth day, of the people of Israel, of the tribe of Benjamin, a Hebrew born of Hebrews; as to the law a Pharisee, as to zeal a persecutor of the church, as to righteousness under the law blameless. But whatever gain I had, I counted as loss for the sake of Christ. Indeed I count everything as loss because of the surpassing worth of knowing Christ Jesus my Lord. For his sake I have suffered the loss of all things, and count them as refuse, in order that I may gain Christ and be found in him, not having a righteousness of my own, based on law, but that which is through faith in Christ, the righteousness from God that depends on faith; that I may know him and the power of his resurrec-

tion, and may share his sufferings, becoming like him in his death, that if possible I may attain the resurrection from the dead.

Philippians 3 vs. 4-11

Down through the ages countless men and women have proved the same thing true. You may never have heard the name of John Newton but few people have missed the song he wrote out of deep experience.

Amazing grace ! How sweet the sound
That saved a wretch like me.
I once was lost, but now am found,
Was blind, but now I see. [6]

Born in 1725 with the privilege of a good home his life became a mess and like the Prodigal son he went into the far country. A biographer tells of his reckless life at sea when he engaged in the African slave trade 'where his conduct awakened, even among the slaves emotions of alarm and astonishment. At home, abroad, on the mighty deep, or on foreign shores, he carried with him the marks of his servitude, the taint of his corruption, and the visible wrath of an offended God'.

Returning from one of his journeys his ship was nearly wrecked off the coast of Ireland. He tells in his own words the experience he had :

The 21st of March is a day much to be remembered by me, and I have never suffered it to pass wholly unnoticed since the year 1748. On that day the Lord sent from on high, and delivered me out of deep waters. I began to think of my former religious professions; the extraordinary turns in my life; the calls, warnings, and deliverances I had met with; the licentious course of my conversation, particularly my unparalleled effrontery in making the gospel-history the constant subject of profane ridicule. I thought, allowing the Scripture premises, there never was, nor could be such a sinner as myself; and, then, comparing the advantages I had broken through, I concluded at first, that my sins were too great to be forgiven. Thus, as I have said, I waited with fear and impatience to receive my inevitable doom. Yet, though I had thoughts of this kind, they were exceedingly faint and disproportionate; it was not till long after (perhaps several years), till I had gained some clear views of the infinite righteousness and grace of Jesus Christ my Lord, that I had a deep and strong apprehension of my state by nature and practice: and, perhaps, till then I could not have borne the sight. When I saw, beyond all probability, there was still hope of respite, and heard about six in the evening that the ship was freed from water, there arose a gleam of hope; I thought I saw the hand of God displayed in our favour. I began to pray; I could not utter the prayer of faith; I could not draw near to a reconciled God, and call him Father. My prayer was like the cry of the ravens, which yet the Lord does not disdain to hear. I now began to think of that Jesus whom I had so often derided. I recollected the particulars of his life, and of his death; and death for sins not his own, but, as I remembered, for the sake of those who in their distress should put their trust in Him. And now I chiefly wanted evidence. The comfortless principles of infidelity were deeply riveted, and I rather wished than believed these things were real facts. The great question now was, how to obtain faith ? I speak not of an appropriating faith (of which I then knew neither the nature nor necessity), but how I should gain an assurance that the Scriptures were of divine inspiration, and a sufficient warrant for the exercise of trust and hope in God. One of the first helps I received (in consequence of a determination to examine the New Testament more carefully) was from Luke 11 v. 13:

'If you then, who are evil, know how to give good gifts to your children, how much more will the heavenly Father give the Holy Spirit to those who ask him!'

I had been sensible that to profess faith in Jesus Christ, when in reality I did not believe his history, was no better than a mockery of a heart-searching God: but here I found a Spirit spoken of, which was to be communicated to those who ask it. Upon this I reasoned thus. If this book is true, the promise in this passage is true likewise. I have need of that very Spirit by which the whole was written, in order to understand it aright. He has engaged here to give that Spirit to those who ask. I must, therefore, pray for it; and if it is of God, he will make good his own word. My purpose was strengthened by John 7 v. 17:

'If any man's will is to do his will, he shall know whether the teaching is from God or whether I am speaking on my own authority.'

I concluded from thence, that though I could not say from my heart that I believed the gospel, yet I would for the present take it for granted, and that by studying it in this light I should be more and more confirmed in it ... Upon the gospel scheme I saw at least a peradventure of hope, but on every other side I was surrounded with black unfathomable despair ... Thus far I was answered, that before we arrived in Ireland I had a satisfactory evidence in my own mind of the truth of the gospel, as considered in itself, and its exact suitableness to answer all my needs. I saw that, by the way there pointed out, God might declare, not his mercy only, but his justice also, in the pardon of sin, on account of the obedience and sufferings of Jesus Christ.[7]

After many years experience in pastoral counselling, meeting people with a wide variety of problems I am convinced that one of the greatest needs which man has is to know his sins forgiven. To offer anyone less than God's almighty power to take away their sin and guilt is to give a stone instead of bread and too often we have been guilty of this in the Church. Reconciliation is costly —it cost the Son of God His life. Long before Christ came Isaiah foresaw this as the ministry of the suffering servant.

Surely he has borne our griefs and carried our sorrows; yet we esteemed him stricken, smitten by God, and afflicted. But he was wounded for our transgressions, he was bruised for our iniquities; upon him was the chastisement that made us whole, and with his stripes we are healed. All we like sheep have gone astray; we have turned every one to his own way; and the Lord has laid on him the iniquity of us all.

Through Christ's death and resurrection there is healing for all the hurts and wounds that our sins and the sins of others have inflicted. Very often in Ireland especially salvation has been presented as a 'fire-escape from Hell' rather than 'wholeness of life'. ' I am come' said Jesus 'that they might have life and have it in all its fullness.'

In my pastoral work I frequently meet people who have such an image of God as an awful ogre that they find it hard to see God revealed in Christ as the one who longs to forgive and reconcile them with Himself. Long before Christ came to reveal God's heart of love the

Psalmist had a profound insight into this truth.

> The Lord is merciful and gracious, slow to anger
> and abounding in steadfast love. He will not
> always chide, nor will he keep his anger for ever.
> He does not deal with us according to our sins,
> nor requite us according to our iniquities. For as
> the heavens are high above the earth, so great is
> his steadfast love toward those who fear him; as
> far as the east is from the west, so far does he
> he remove our transgressions from us. As a
> father pities his children, so the Lord pities those
> who fear him. For he knows our frame; he
> remembers that we are dust.
>
> Psalm 103 vs. 8-14

In his commentary on these verses Matthew Henry
observes :

> Our crimes were capital, but God saves our lives
> by pardoning them; our diseases were mortal but
> God saves our lives by healing them. If God
> takes away the guilt of sin by pardoning mercy
> He will break the power of sin by renewing
> grace.

Like Saint Paul and John Newton I too must come to
receive this reconciliation if I am to know that peace with
God which they found. Others may help me on that road
but there comes that moment of encounter which issues
in new birth, new joy, new life and an awareness that God
is truly my Father and I am his son. I know, not just with
my heart and my whole being that God loves me.

Recently I spent several hours praying with someone
who was going through a difficult time of mental anguish
and, as frequently happens his mind had pushed some of
the suffering into his body and he was in great pain with
stomach ulcers. As I laid hands on him and prayed the
Lord powerfully ministered to him. As he left me he said

'I feel I have been born all over again, a great burden has fallen off my shoulders.' Such is the power of God's reconciling love that all the disintegration of my life is brought into a harmony that issues in great joy. This was well illustrated by another incident which happened to a postman in Limerick some time ago. A group of Christians had prayed with him on Sunday night that he might experience the infilling of God's Holy Spirit. On the Monday morning as he went on his rounds he suddenly felt so overwhelmed with the love of God for him that he had to get off his bicycle and just stand on the roadside drinking in the wonder of it all. Then the joy of this new awareness so possessed him that he left down his bicycle and did cartwheel hand turns down the road ! Was he not entering into the experience of the Psalmist who declared with great joy?

> Thou hast turned for me my mourning into dancing; thou hast loosed my sackcloth and girded me with gladness, that my soul may praise thee and not be silent. O Lord my God, I will give thanks to thee for ever.
>
> Psalm 30 vs. 11 & 12

I sought the Lord, and afterward I knew
He moved my soul to seek Him, seeking me;
It was not I that found, O Saviour true—
No, I was found by Thee.
Thou didst reach forth thy hand and mine
   enfold;
I walked and sank not on the storm-vexed sea,—
'Twas not so much that I on Thee took hold,
As Thou, dear Lord, on me.
I find, I walk, I love, but O the whole
Of love is but my answer, Lord, to Thee;
For thou wast long beforehand with my soul,
Alway Thou lovedst me.[8]

(1) From hymn *It is a Thing Most Wonderful*. Bishop W. Walsham How.

(2) From hymn *There is a Green Hill Far Away*. Mrs. Cecil F. Alexander.

(3) *And can it be that I should gain*. Charles Wesley.

(4) *There's a Way Back to God*. E. H. Swinstead.

(5) From *And can it be that I should gain*. Charles Wesley.

(6) *Amazing Grace!* John Newton.

(7) From *A Life of the Rev. John Newton* as quoted in *The Works of William Cowper*. William Tegg & Co., London 1851.

(8) *I sought the Lord, and Afterward I knew*. Anon.

For Your Meditation

And you he made alive, when you were dead
through the trespasses and sins in which you once
walked, following the course of this world,
following the prince of the power of the air, the
spirit that is now at work in the sons of disobedience. Among these we all once lived in the
passions of our flesh, following the desires of
body and mind, and so we were by nature
children of wrath, like the rest of mankind. But
God, who is rich in mercy, out of the great love
with which he loved us, even when we were dead
through our trespasses, made us alive together
with Christ (by grace you have been saved), and
raised us up with him, and made us sit with him
in the heavenly places in Christ Jesus, that in the
coming ages he might show the immeasurable
riches of his grace in kindness toward us in
Christ Jesus. For by grace you have been saved
through faith; and this is not your own doing, it
is the gift of God—not because of works, lest
any man should boast. For we are his workman-
ship, created in Christ Jesus for good works,
which God prepared beforehand, that we should
walk in them.

Ephesians 2 vs. 1-10

A Prayer

And so, from the day we heard of it, we have
not ceased to pray for you, asking that you may
be filled with the knowledge of his will in all
spiritual wisdom and understanding, to lead a
life worthy of the Lord, fully pleasing to him,
bearing fruit in every good work and increasing
in the knowledge of God. May you be strengthened with all power, according to his glorious
might, for all endurance and patience with joy,
giving thanks to the Father, who has qualified
us to share in the inheritance of the saints in
light. He has delivered us from the dominion of
darkness and transferred us to the kingdom of
his beloved Son, in whom we have redemption,
the forgiveness of sins.

Colossians 1 vs. 9-14

5. The Dividing Wall is Broken

Through the reconciling work of Christ on the Cross I am set free from sin and fear and death. The barriers between me and God are removed and fellowship is stored. That is the 'vertical' dimension of the Cross. But the horizontal dimension follows the vertical as night follows day.

In Christ's death I am reconciled to the Father but also made one with all those who have like me received by faith that reconciliation. As I kneel at the foot of the Cross and stretch out my hands to receive the gift of salvation which God in His mercy and grace offers me I realise that my hands are touching the hands of others who are kneeling there too. And as I kneel there I realise that I have nothing over those who are there with me and they have nothing over me. This has profound significance for all my relationships with other Christians 'saved by grace'. When we kneel at the Cross to receive the reconciliation of Christ the Roman Catholic has nothing over the Anglican, the Anglican has nothing over the Presbyterian and the Methodist has nothing over the Congregationalist. And when we receive that reconciliation which we could neither earn nor achieve we are united inseparably to all who have received that reconciliation with us.

When this truth dawns on us it brings at first a great

shock but then a great release in joy, to realise that we suddenly have acquired a host of new brothers and sisters in the Lord. To know that:

We are heirs of the Father
We are joint heirs with the Son
We are children of the Kingdom
We are family, we are one.[1]

It was this great truth which became a living experience for the Christians of the first century. A whole new concept of brotherhood was introduced into the world. A brotherhood which transcended the barriers of race, colour and nationality. For those early Christians brought up in the Jewish tradition this was a devastating truth to accept. They were the chosen people and thought that God had little interest in others.

From the earliest moment it became clear that Christ's ministry was to reveal God's love and make it available to men and women all over the world. Old Simeon in the Temple was inspired to speak these words when Jesus was brought there by his parents for the dedication service:

Lord, now lettest thou thy servant depart in peace, according to thy word; for mine eyes have seen thy salvation which thou hast prepared in the presence of all peoples, a light for revelation to the Gentiles, and for glory to thy people Israel.

Saint Luke vs. 29-32

When the Lord began his public ministry Saint Luke tells us that after he read from the book of Isaiah:

'The Spirit of the Lord is upon me, because he has anointed me to preach good news to the poor. He has sent me to proclaim release to the captives and recovering of sight to the blind, to

set at liberty those who are oppressed, to proclaim the acceptable year of the Lord.' And he
closed the book, and gave it back to the attend-
ant, and sat down; and the eyes of all in the
synagogue were fixed on him. And he began to
say to them, 'Today this scripture has been
fulfilled in your hearing.'

Saint Luke 4 vs. 18-21

When they heard this there was spontaneous
applause 'all spoke well of him and wondered at the
gracious words that proceeded from his mouth'. But when
He went on to speak about God blessing and using people
like a 'widow from Sidon' and 'A Syrian soldier like
Naaman' their deep prejudice and awful anger was
aroused. To think that he could even mention 'these
foreigners' in their synagogue was too much for them and
they did their best to lynch Him.

When they heard this, all in the synagogue were
filled with wrath. And they rose up and put him
out of the city, and led him to the brow of the
hill on which their city was built, that they
might throw him down headlong. But passing
through the midst of them he went away.

Saint Luke 4 vs. 28-30

The whole of our Lord's ministry and life was a
judgment on narrow-mindedness, pride and prejudice. He
was the really free man. Free from the fear of men which
so often prevents us speaking the truth. Free from the
prejudice which so often prevents us from seeing another
man as he really is. Free from the pride which so often
prevents us from giving and receiving the forgiveness
which we need in healing relationships.

How misleading the image of Jesus can be for many
people, coloured as it is by pictures of Him in spotless

robes and with unruffled hair moving among well-behaved children and fishermen in their Sunday suits. The modern portrayal of Jesus as the 'superstar' moving fanatically among hysterical fans is no more helpful.

It is good to remind ourselves that Jesus lived in an atmosphere of political intrigue, civil strife and brutal violence not unlike what we have experienced over the past years in Northern Ireland. A victim of discrimination 'with a manger for a bed' at the moment of His birth He was brought up in the sectarian ghetto of Galilee among the poorest of the poor. The tramping boots of the Roman legions along the Western road was a familiar sound of His early childhood. His country was occupied by a foreign power and he must have become very familiar with feelings of bitterness which had entered into the lives of his fellow countrymen. The strains of the nationalist songs would often have reached his ears of 'A nation once again', 'Ourselves alone', 'A King and our Kingdom', 'For God and Israel'. The wall slogans that accompany the feelings of despair and hatred must often have been before him. The freedom fighters of Northern Galilee were notorious. Indeed one of them Simon the Zealot became His disciple. Many of his school friends would have been tempted to join the para-military organisations of the day. There was no television then to bring the news of new atrocities before the eyes of the people— an even more sinister visual reminder was provided. Along the public roads the bodies of guerilla fighters would be crucified by the Roman soldiers and left for days as a grim reminder to the passers by. These were the grim realities that existed in the world in which Jesus lived. There must always have been the temptation to speak for 'his people' to make statements about the oppressed and the oppressors, to take sides. And this He refused to do for they were all alike God's children and

He wanted them to find a way to live together instead of destroying one another. Once after the miracle of the feeding of the five thousand the crowd became wild with excitement and tried to force him to become their King but John tells us 'He withdrew to the hills by himself'.

He was no dreamer, no starry-eyed idealist. He knew what was in man but He also saw what man could become by the power of God working in him. What a difficult task our Lord set Himself when He gathered the twelve to be His disciples, men with such different personalities and backgrounds, such varied hopes and aspirations. Simon the Zealot, a former guerilla fighter working alongside Matthew, the tax collector, the man who had played into the hands of the 'enemy' by collecting taxes for them. James and John, 'the sons of thunder' who seriously talked of a 'scorched-earth policy' and were ready to burn down the Samaritan village where the people would not entertain Jesus and His disciples. Peter, the blustering man of action who carried a dagger beneath his cloak and used it in the Garden of Gethsemane when the armed guard came to arrest Jesus. It was men like these who were changed by the reconciling power and love of Christ. To such hard-headed men with such diverse experience of life Jesus was able to impart such incredible teaching as this:

> You have heard that it was said, 'An eye for an eye and a tooth for a tooth.' But I say to you, Do not resist one who is evil. But if any one strikes you on the right cheek, turn to him the other also; and if any one would sue you and take your coat, let him have your cloak as well; and if any one forces you to go one mile, go with him two miles. Give to him who begs from you, and do not refuse him who would borrow from you. 'You have heard that it was said,

"You shall love your neighbour and hate your enemy." But I say to you, Love your enemies and pray for those who persecute you, so that you may be sons of your Father who is in heaven; for he makes his sun rise on the evil and on the good, and sends rain on the just and on the unjust. For if you love those who love you, what reward have you? Do not even the tax collectors do the same? And if you salute only your brethren, what more are you doing than others? Do not even the Gentiles do the same? You, therefore, must be perfect, as your heavenly Father is perfect.'

Saint Matthew 5 vs. 38-48

We can just imagine how incredibly difficult it was for those disciples to take what Jesus was saying. Once Peter came to Him for explanation of this new quality of forgiveness about which Jesus talked. 'How often must I forgive my brother if he wrongs me? As often as seven times?' Jesus answered 'Not seven, I tell you, but seventy times seven'. And to drive home his message the Lord went on to tell the story of the unforgiving debtor.

Therefore the kingdom of heaven may be compared to a king who wished to settle accounts with his servants. When he began the reckoning, one was brought to him who owed him ten thousand talents; and as he could not pay, his lord ordered him to be sold, with his wife and children and all that he had, and payment to be made. So the servant fell on his knees, imploring him, 'Lord, have patience with me, and I will pay you everything.' And out of pity for him the lord of that servant released him and forgave him the debt. But that same servant, as he went out, came upon one of his fellow servants who owed him a hundred denarii; and seizing him by the throat he said, 'Pay what you owe'. So his fellow servant fell down and besought him, 'Have patience with me, and I will pay you.' He refused and went and put him in prison till he should pay the debt. When his fellow servants saw what had taken place, they were greatly distressed, and they went and reported to their lord all that had taken place. Then his lord summoned him and said to him, 'You wicked servant! I forgave you all that debt because you besought me; and should not you have had mercy on your fellow servant, as I had mercy on you?' And in anger his lord delivered him to the jailers, till he should pay all his debt. So also my heavenly Father will do to every one of you, if you do not forgive your brother from your heart.

Saint Matthew 18 vs. 23-38

All this talk about love and forgiveness might have sounded fine on the flower-covered fields of Galilee. It is easy enough to talk like that when all is going well. And how often we have listened to those words from a Church pulpit or lectern. It is quite another matter when it comes to the hard reality of meeting the brother who does you wrong and despitefully uses and abuses you. For Christ the test was soon to come and in the laboratory of living experience He proved the theories true. It does work. Love heals. Love saves. Love to the uttermost creates the miracle. A way is opened through the dark morass of endless conflict and hatred into brotherhood and love.

When human pride and intrigue and naked hatred had joined to hound Him to a cruel death by crucifixion in His moment of great agony He called out 'Father, forgive them, for they know not what they do.'

Their foolish stubborn pride and blind prejudice could not tolerate a man who could not be conveniently pigeon-holed. As Jesus hung there on the Cross with arms outstretched to all the world he offered man not only a way back to God but also to real acceptance into the human family without fear or favour. It is no accident that the first two people to receive the reconciliation of the Cross were the dying 'freedom fighter' who hung beside the Lord and the Roman soldier who exclaimed 'Truly this was the Son of God'. Two sworn enemies reconciled by the power of Christ's redeeming love. Here was a power released that would melt the most intractable barriers that separate man from God and man from man and here is the only way of reconciliation for a broken and divided world.

It was this quality of reconciling love expressed in the lives of the Christians that made such an impression on the pagan world of the first century.

> Bless those who persecute you, bless and do not curse them. Rejoice with those who rejoice, weep with those who weep. Live in harmony with one another; do not be haughty, but associate with the lowly; never be conceited. Repay no one evil for evil, but take thought for what is noble in the sight of all. If possible, so far as it depends upon you, live peaceably with all. Beloved, never avenge yourselves, but leave it to the wrath of God; for it is written, 'Vengeance is mine, I will repay, says the Lord.' No, 'if your enemy is hungry, feed him; if he is thirsty, give him drink; for by so doing you will heap burning coals upon his head.' Do not be overcome by evil, but overcome evil with good.

> Romans 12 vs. 14-21

Those incredible words were written by a man who once stood by and consented to the murder of the first Christian martyr Saint Stephen. As he stood there by the roadside and watched as his friends and accomplices cruelly stoned Stephen to death Saul, full of hated, bitterness and revenge began to see the reconciling love of Jesus. For as Stephen died in agony, instead of cursing Saul, Stephen prayed with a radiant glory shining from his blood-stained face. 'Lord Jesus, do not lay this sin to their charge'. I venture to believe that experience was the first step on the road to making Paul, the former Saul of Tarsus, the greatest missionary the Christian Church has ever known.

This deep problem of hatred and bitterness which Saul of Tarsus had inherited and which had been fed by his strict training in religious Judaism was challenged to the very roots. He was forced to re-think the whole of his approach to life and the Christian way. In his Damascus road experience he had a personal encounter with Christ so deep and real that his whole life was turned upside down. What happened immediately after that is of great significance. Those who would have had most cause to fear this 'persecutor of the Christians' were the very ones who extended to him the right hand of friendship and welcomed him into the fellowship of the Christian Church.

For three days after his dramatic experience on the Damascus Road Saul sat blind and hungry and alone in the house of Judas in Straight Street, Damascus. It was a little known disciple named Ananias who was the agent of reconciliation for Saul. In a vision God had spoken to Ananias and asked him to go and meet this man. We can feel the consternation and confusion which Ananias felt and his reaction was a very natural one.

But Ananias answered, 'Lord, I have heard from many about this man, how much evil he has done to thy saints at Jerusalem.'

Acts 9 v. 13

Ananias obeyed and I never fail to be moved at the greeting with which he addressed Saul. There before him was the great enemy of the Church who had come to arrest, torture and imprison the Christians and Ananias's first words to him were 'Brother Saul'. Is it any wonder that when he laid his hands of healing on Saul's head 'immediately something like scales fell from Saul's eyes' and he regained his sight. I cannot help feeling that the scales which fell from his eyes were the filaments of prejudice, hatred and fear which for so long had blinded Saul to the real truth about Christ's all embracing love for all men.

A further incident was to confirm for Saul the power of Christ to break down the walls of hate and fear. When he came to Jerusalem after his conversion there was understandable suspicion about his motives. Luke records that 'when he came to Jerusalem, he tried to join the disciples, but they were all afraid of him, not believing that he really was a disciple. It was Barnabas, 'the son of encouragement' who took Saul by the right hand and introduced him to the fearful Christians as a new brother in the Lord.

By the power of Christ's reconciling love the impossible had happened. The proud Jew now became 'the apostle of the Gentiles'. The love of Christ mediated through Stephen, Ananias and Barnabas had melted the hard heart and released Saul from the narrow boundaries of sectarianism to become Paul, the greatest Christian missionary of all time.

Years later when writing to the Christians in Ephesus

he outlined the great truth of Christ's power to break down the barriers that divide man from God and man from man.

> Therefore remember that at one time you Gentiles in the flesh, called the uncircumcision by what is called the circumcision, which is made in the flesh by hands—remember that you were at that time separated from Christ, alienated from the commonwealth of Israel, and strangers to the covenants of promise, having no hope and without God in the world. But now in Christ Jesus you who once were far off have been brought near in the blood of Christ. For He is our peace, who has made us both one, and has broken down the dividing wall of hostility, by abolishing in his flesh the law of commandments and ordinances, that he might create in himself one new man in place of the two, so making peace, and might reconcile us both to God in one body through the Cross, thereby bringing the hostility to an end. And he came and preached peace to you who were far off and peace to those who were near; for through him we both have access in one Spirit to the Father.
>
> Ephesians 2 vs. 11-18

It is this text which has become a foundation one for our work in the Christian Renewal Centre which was established in 1974 in Rostrevor near the border between the Republic of Ireland and Northern Ireland. 'Christ Himself is our way of peace'. It is through His power alone that all the barriers of hatred can be melted away. Because we have seen this happen in Ireland between those who have been separated for centuries from one another we believe that what has happened to the few can happen to all when we are prepared to kneel together at the foot of the Cross. What it will mean for us will be no less than it was for Saint Paul in the humiliation which forgiveness demanded. Its consequences will be no less liberating either as the scales of fear and prejudice fall from our eyes and we are able to recognise and embrace one another as brothers. One of the greatest miracles in my life has been this experience becoming a reality for me in relation especially to Roman Catholics.

Anyone born in Northern Ireland is born with prejudice in his bloodstream. Fed by ignorance, fear and separation it becomes a hard wall of suspicion and hatred, which from time to time erupts into awful violence and incredible brutality. Several years ago Dr. G. B. Newe expressed a truth which many of us find hard to credit or understand 'We have been more cruel, more hurting, more unkind to one another than any invader could be. The harsh reality is that more harm has been done to the Irish nation, North and South in the past few years than any invader would have dared to do to us'.

How can such a state of affairs be explained? How can such apparently friendly people be so bitter towards one another? In order to understand the root of bitterness that lies deep in the hearts of many Irishmen it is necessary to go back three hundred years. In a very real way we have become 'prisoners of the past' and without doubt we are experiencing 'the sins of the fathers being visited on the children to the third and fourth generation'.

I can only speak personally and illustrate from my own experience what must be the experience of many in Ireland. I was brought up in a rural part of Northern Ireland in a community which is almost equally Roman Catholic and Protestant. Like most Protestants in Northern Ireland my forebears had come over from Scotland

and England in the early 17th century during the Plantation under James I. When they came they took over the good land from the native Irish who were largely Roman Catholics. When they took Joe's land from him he had to go to the hills and the bogs and eke out a living there as best he could. They set to work with energy and enthusiasm to make their new home. They built a sturdy house and a high wall around it to protect their family and to let the 'natives' know that the land had new owners. I can take it that Joe was not exactly delighted with his new neighbours. Indeed resentment quickly built into anger and anger led to action and he did everything he could to drive them out. Quick-witted and with a good knowledge of the countryside he became more and more adept at producing schemes for their destruction, while they used all their skill and power to outwit him. If he came to their window at night with his knife drawn to kill them they drew their guns from under their pillows and disposed of him first. In time they strengthened their position in solidarity with their planter neighbours. Joe and his friends realised that they were not going to get rid of my forebears so easily and in order to make a tolerable living they offered to come and work for them. It was humiliating for Joe but he saw no other way out of it. They got to know him better—he was a good herdsman and did a fair day's work and they gave him more responsibility. But one thing they would never do was to TRUST HIM. Under no circumstances could he share the land with them. His intention was to wrest it from them: though they knew him well they must never fully TRUST HIM—and the feeling was mutual. That was three hundred years ago but it might have been yesterday. That invisible wall of mistrust has remained over the centuries only becoming visible when circumstances combine to bring hostility into open conflict such as we have had for the past seven years. To the onlooker Joe and I appear good friends—we work together on many projects. We can serve on agricultural committees, we can even meet together for all kinds of social activities. We may even attend religious services together but in the end of the day deep down there is that invisible barrier of mistrust lodged deep within our hearts like a steel shutter which extends to an area of the brain and cuts off from rational argument and discussion. Deep down it is this which stands in the way of 'power-sharing' and co-operation at a level where I am threatened on the point of my existence. Catholic insistence on equal shares arouses the centuries-old demon of fear in the Protestant mind— a fear which for him spells complete disaster for if what he has taken is wrested from him he has nowhere to turn. The Catholic still has his house on the hill. 'What we have we hold' and 'Not an inch' are not just silly slogans— they are pregnant with meaning for a Protestant whose very identity and existence seem threatened. Equally the Catholic feels the desperation of his fate—that he is to be eternally assigned a second-class ticket—always in the position of being told to stay in his place by a paternalism, however benign that master might become.

This is the root of the problem and it is a root firmly grounded in the hard earth of Irish soil. All attempts to reach political solutions must take cognizance of this fact. And it is precisely here where politics or any man-made solution will always fail. There is urgent need for political solutions to the problems of this land and we should constantly pray for those who have the enormous burden of working out such solutions. The more fundamental problem needs more basic remedies. The heart must be changed and I know only one power that can change the human heart—the power of God through the reconciling love of Jesus Christ.

It's not enough just to move the furniture around, it's

not enough just to change the structures—the past few years should surely have convinced us of that. You cannot have a new Ireland without new Irishmen and only God can make new Irishmen.

This is what God is able to do by His Spirit in our land today. As I speak with our politicians and hear them talk I realise the awful dilemma they are in. It's like a log jam and they cannot find a way out. And there is no way out till we can forgive one another and accept one another. And we cannot forgive one another till we allow God to forgive us. This is at once the simplest and yet the most difficult thing we shall be called on to do. But if we do not do it we perish. We must find a way to live together or we shall die together.

In ordinary human relations, for example in a marriage, we know how difficult it is to forgive—I suppose the hardest sentence we ever say is 'I'm sorry' but till that is done there is no future for a real relationship. When it's done there's no limit to the future that is before us.

I firmly believe, because I know it in my own experience and in the experience of many others that God can come in the power of His Holy Spirit and so work in my heart that He can melt away the hatred of the centuries and give me ground for hope and trust. He can liberate me from the prison houses of the past into a far more glorious future. On both sides the tragedy is that with closed and clenched fists we are holding onto the past which is dead and gone. We worship it with a fanatical devotion. Only when we open our hands can we grasp the future. Hatred destroys the one who hates as much as it destroys the one who is hated. Clenched fists even if they are never used in combat become cold and rock like.

I need a power to come within my heart to give the warmth to allow my hands to open. When I encounter the risen Christ I see the open hands which were pierced with nails for me and for Joe and for Mary and I can ask Him to release me and set me free. There is no other way. This is asking for a miracle. It has happened and it is happening, as all over the land men and women are finding a unity at the Cross which takes away their fear and sets them free. At the height of the violence in Belfast I remember one evening when a group of us, from Roman Catholic and Protestant traditions, were gathered together for prayer a very clear picture flashed into my mind of a little tree growing at the base of a high wall. It was a hard, cold wall like so many of the walls on which slogans of hate are printed. I shared the 'vision' with the others in the group and a young geology student was there who said: 'The greatest power is the power of living tissue. In time as the roots of that little tree go down deep into the soil of God's marvellous love the hatred of centuries can be melted away.'

Even in the midst of the awful agony of human suffering the miracle of reconciling love has been repeated time and time again in Northern Ireland. What has constantly inspired me over the past years has been the fact that those who have suffered most have often been those who are most ready to forgive. I'm thinking now of the young social worker who was a victim of a terrible disaster in the centre of Belfast. Joan had just dropped into the Abercorn Restaurant for a Saturday afternoon cup of tea when a bomb was planted and she was blown through the ceiling. She lost a leg and an eye and suffered multiple injuries. After fighting a grim battle with death for a fortnight in the intensive care unit of the Royal Victoria Hospital she spent over a year in hospital. Just before her release from hospital as she waited for her artificial leg to be fitted I remember talking over the experiences she had gone through in those early weeks of intense agony which she had suffered and when we had ministered to her. I asked her how she felt towards those who planted the bomb and she said: 'I have no hatred in my heart.'

Or I think of the blind father of the young fireman who was shot dead just a few hundred yards from our house in Belfast when he was fighting a blaze. Interviewed on the radio a few days later the grief-stricken father who had depended so much on his son said: 'I don't feel hatred for those who killed my son. I feel so sorry for them and I'm praying for them.' A doctor whose son was gunned down beside him in the car as he drove the boy to school was heard to pray 'Father, forgive them' as he lay in a hospital bed recovering from the injuries which he had sustained in the attack.

Another incident which illustrates the healing of forgiving love was related to me by Fanny Robertson, one of the members of our community in the Christian Renewal Centre, who worked in Belfast until recently:

> For some time a group of Catholics and Protestants have been meeting for prayer each Sunday evening on the verge of a bitterly divided district. One evening last winter I arrived rather late, having come from my own Presbyterian evening service. As I entered the room I noticed, rather vaguely, a sad-looking woman dressed in unrelieved black. I did not remember having seen her before, and wondered who she was.
>
> When the meeting ended, and we were drinking a cup of tea and chatting together, one of the Catholic leaders came over and asked me if I would join him to pray with someone. It was the lady in black. As I sat down beside her I asked her what she wanted us to pray for. She explained that her brother had been assassinated the previous Monday evening. She had felt restless and unhappy at home, and then she remembered this prayer group would be meeting, and decided to come along. Then she said, 'I want

someone from both communities to pray for me —a Catholic like myself and a Protestant—that there may be no bitterness in me.' I was touched, yet thrilled, by her attitude.

So a Catholic businessman, and a Presbyterian woman, together gently laid our hands on her, and prayed—for forgiveness for those in both communities who could act so brutally, for forgiveness for ourselves for anything we might have contributed to the situation, and for freedom from bitterness for us all. Then we committed her lovingly to the God of all comfort. Our prayer for her was answered. I met her a few months later, a regular member of that and other groups meeting for shared prayer, quietly ministering similar healing to other hurt and confused members of our broken society.

Even in the darkest moments of the past years in Ireland when the ominous clouds of despair have crept upon us I have been sustained by the witness of countless lives of ordinary Christians who have reflected the hope of resurrection. The noise of the bombs and bullets may often daunt us into despair. The hateful invective of the sick and fearful politicians may constantly catch the headlines but behind those headlines there is endless testimony to the power of love to heal, to endure and in the end to win the final victory.

It was in a little church right in the heart of Northern Ireland where some terrible violence had occurred that I was given a living parable that I shall always hold before me. In that area of great tension two hundred people had come together from all parts of Ireland—North and South, Roman Catholic and Protestant—for a memorable week-end of prayer and study. Miracles of reconciliation had occurred during that time as people had met each other as brothers and sisters in Christ from across the divide of centuries. The rector of the church had asked me to preach the sermon at the service where the local congregation was joined by the visitors from such varied backgrounds. I wanted to speak on Christ's power to reconcile and just as I mounted the pulpit steps I was given a remarkable parable in the window just beside the pulpit. The stained glass in the window had been shattered by a recent explosion in the telephone exchange next door to the church. Of the three panels in the upper part of the window only two remained intact. They depicted faith and love. Hope had gone. It had been blown out of the window — just as it had been quite literally for thousands of people in our war-torn country. But as I reflected on that picture before me I realised what God was saying to us on that morning. If our faith is together placed in the crucified and risen Lord Jesus Christ and we allow Him by the power of His Spirit to pour His love into our hearts then hope will return. 'Faith, hope and love and the greatest of these is love.' These are the qualities that are eternal. They are ours in Christ and nothing can take them from us.

> Who shall separate us from the love of Christ ? Shall tribulation, or distress, or persecution, or famine, or nakedness, or peril, or sword ? As it is written, 'For thy sake we are being killed all the day long; we are regarded as sheep to be slaughtered.' No, in all these things we are more than conquerors through him who loved us. For I am sure that neither death, nor life, nor angels, nor principalities, nor things present, nor things to come, nor powers, nor height, nor depth, nor anything else in all creation, will be able to separate us from the love of God in Christ Jesus our Lord.

Romans 8 vs. 35-39

An assassin's bullet killed Martin Luther King on April 4th, 1968. The youngest Nobel Prize winner in history, he was 39 at the time of his death. Fourteen years earlier when he became involved in the struggle for civil rights for American negroes he had no idea where his work of reconciliation would lead him and how costly it would be. After a period of constant disturbance of his family from malicious telephone callers he was tempted to give it all up and fall quietly back into an easier life. He tells of the tension he experienced at that time and of how he responded to the clear call of God in his moment of anguish and near despair.

After a particularly strenuous day, I settled in bed at a late hour. My wife had already fallen asleep and I was about to doze off when the telephone rang. An angry voice said, 'Listen, nigger, we've taken all we want from you. Before next week you'll be sorry you ever came to Montgomery.' I hung up, but I could not sleep. It seemed that all of my fears had come down on me at once. I had reached the saturation point.

I got out of bed and began to walk the floor. Finally, I went to the kitchen and heated a pot of coffee. I was ready to give up. I tried to think of a way to move out of the picture without appearing to be a coward. In this state of exhaustion, when my courage had almost gone, I determined to take my problem to God. My head in my hands, I bowed over the kitchen table and prayed aloud. The words I spoke to God that midnight are still vivid in my memory. 'I am here taking a stand for what I believe is right. But now I am afraid. The people are looking to me for leadership, and if I stand before them without strength and courage, they too will falter. I am at the end of my powers. I have nothing left. I've come to the point where I can't face it alone.'

At that moment I experienced the presence of the Divine as I had never before experienced him. It seemed as though I could hear the quiet assurance of an inner voice, saying, 'Stand up for righteousness, stand up for truth. God will be at your side forever.' Almost at once my fears began to pass from me. My uncertainty disappeared. I was ready to face anything. The outer situation remained the same, but God had given me an inner calm.

Three nights later, our home was bombed. Strangely enough, I accepted the word of the bombing calmly. My experience with God had given me a new strength and trust. I knew now that God is able to give us the interior resources to face the storms and problems of life.[2]

[1] From *If My People*.

[2] *Strength to Love*. Page 113. By Martin Luther King. Fontana Books.

For Your Meditation

If then you have been raised with Christ, seek the things that are above, where Christ is, seated at the right hand of God. Set your minds on things that are above, not on things that are on earth. For you have died, and your life is hid with Christ in God. When Christ who is our life appears, then you also will appear with him in glory. Put to death therefore what is earthly in you: fornication, impurity, passion, evil desire, and covetousness, which is idolatry. On account of these the wrath of God is coming. In these you once walked, when you lived in them. But now put them all away: anger, wrath, malice, slander, and foul talk from your mouth. Do not lie to one another, seeing that you have put off the old nature with its practices and have put on the new nature, which is being renewed in knowledge after the image of its creator. Here there cannot be Greek and Jew, circumcised and uncircumcised, barbarian, Scythian, slave, free man. but Christ is all, and in all. Put on then, as God's chosen ones, holy and beloved, compassion, kindness, lowliness, meekness, and patience, forbearing one another and, if one has a complaint against another, forgiving each other; as the Lord has forgiven you, so you also must forgive. And above all these put on love, which binds everything together in perfect harmony. And let the peace of Christ rule in your hearts, to which indeed you were called in the one body. And be thankful. Let the word of Christ dwell in you richly, teach and admonish one another in all wisdom, and sing psalms and hymns and spiritual songs with thankfulness in your hearts to God. And whatever you do, in word or deed, do everything in the name of the Lord Jesus, giving thanks to God the Father through him.

Colossians 3 vs. 1-17

A Prayer

Merciful God, to thee we commend ourselves and all those
who need thy help and correction.
Where there is hatred, give love;
Where there is injury, pardon;
Where there is doubt, faith;
Where there is despair, hope;
Where there is sadness, joy;
Where there is darkness, light.
Grant that we may not seek so much to be consoled, as
to console; to be understood, as to understand;
to be loved, as to love;
For in giving we receive, in pardoning we are pardoned,
and dying we are born into eternal life.

Saint Francis of Assisi.

6. That They May Be One

> So we are ambassadors for Christ, God making His appeal through us. We beseech you on behalf of Christ, be reconciled to God.
>
> 2 Corinthians 5 v. 20

In every day and age this is the high calling of the Christian Church to be agents of His reconciling love. How can we effectively proclaim the reconciliation which God offers in Christ if we are spending our energies in slandering one another. The great scandal of disunity is a major stumbling block to the progress of the Gospel. The tragedy is that in the Churches we are often so complacent about it and spend so much time defending our corners that we let the world with all its need of Christ's reconciling love pass by. It is not unfair to say that so frequently our efforts at ecumenism are little more than window dressing, the pleasant occupation of a few people who can 'pass themselves' with pretended friendship for a week in January and return quickly to their cosy corners. We speak in our prayers about our 'unhappy divisions'. Are we really any happier when we are together? Many of the 'ecumenical' services which I have attended have not been exactly characterised by hilarious joy! When we pray for unity are we really serious? I would venture to suggest that many of us add an inaudible concluding phrase to many prayers for unity—'And not until after my lifetime, Lord, Amen!'

How hypocritical it must sound in the ears of many when from our Churches we call on our politicians to do that which we are not prepared to do. We make impassioned pleas to our political leaders to stretch every nerve to find ways of working together towards a solution of our unhappy divisions. Have they not a perfect right to turn to us and ask us what we are prepared to do about it in our churches? Surely they have the right to say to us 'Put your own house in order'!

It is when we set the realities of some of these local situations alongside some of the statements which have emerged from ecumenical congresses that we might often be tempted to despair. The meeting of the World Council of Churches held in New Delhi in 1961 came up with the excellent definition of the unity we seek:

> We believe that the unity which is both God's will and his gift to his Church is being made visible as all in each place who are baptized into Jesus Christ and confess him as Lord and Saviour are brought by the Holy Spirit into one fully committed fellowship, holding the one apostolic faith, preaching the one Gospel, breaking the one bread, joining in common prayer, and having a corporate life reaching out in witness and service to all, and who at the same time are united with the whole Christian fellowship in all places and all ages in such wise that ministry and members are accepted by all, and that all can act and speak together as occasion requires for the tasks to which God calls his people. [1]

In 1964 five hundred representatives from all the main non-Roman-Catholic Churches in Great Britain met at Nottingham for a Faith and Order Conference and passed this resolution:

United in our urgent desire for One Church Renewed for Mission, this conference invites the member Churches of the British Council of Churches, in appropriate groupings such as nations, to covenant together to work and pray for the inauguration of union by a date agreed among them. We dare to hope that this date should not be later than Easter Day, 1980.[2]

With 1980 fast approaching it is salutary to ask how far the British Churches have come in realising that vision?

In the renewal which the Holy Spirit is bringing in our day I sense a new urgency for an answer to the Lord's Prayer 'that they may become perfectly one' so that the whole world might believe in Christ. It is a marked feature of the Charismatic renewal in every part of the world that Christians are discovering a new sense of unity in the Spirit in the bond of peace. The way in which the Holy Spirit is being poured out today in complete disregard of denominational background is something which many find really exciting and others find impossible to understand. For those who have neatly fitted the Holy Spirit into their framework of theological understanding or ecclesiastical structure it is a devastating realisation. If you believed that the Roman Catholic Church was the sole repository of all truth and outside of its allegiance there was no salvation it is a traumatic experience to ask a Protestant to pray for you that you might be baptized with the Holy Spirit. Yet all over the place this is what is happening. It was through members of the Pentecostal Churches that some of the young Roman Catholics who are now leaders of the Charismatic Renewal in the Roman Catholic Church came into the blessing of the pentecostal experience. In the Republic of Ireland it was a visit by a Presbyterian minister, the Rev. Thomas Smail, in company with a Roman Catholic priest, Fr. Joe McGeedy, that led to the formation of the first charismatic prayer group of twelve students. In three years the movement has grown so much that the weekly meeting in Dublin for shared prayer and praise draws over 700 with numerous smaller meetings all over the city throughout the week. It was through that meeting in Dublin in the summer of 1972 that I was first led into deep fellowship with Roman Catholics in the Spirit of the Lord. When I entered the room in University College where over seventy people were praying and praising God together I was deeply moved. I was moved first by the sense of the presence and peace of Christ which reigned there and secondly by the warmth of Christian love and fellowship which was extended to me. After many years of having engaged in some rather bitter controversy over theological differences I found myself one in the Spirit with many from whom I would have been before estranged. One of the first Roman Catholics in Belfast to be involved in the Charismatic renewal was a businessman who has become to me a dear brother in the Lord. When a Protestant friend first spoke to him about the power of the Holy Spirit he became really interested and asked a Pentecostal pastor to pray with him that he might be 'baptized in the Spirit'. The pastor who was so taken aback that a Roman Catholic should make such a request deferred the decision because he really was not sure that a Roman Catholic was fit material for the blessing! He took a week to think and pray and thank God he came back to pray with him and he received a real infilling of the power of the Holy Spirit. God has used him all over the North of Ireland to spread the Good News of the power of Jesus Christ to save, to heal and to baptize with the Holy Spirit.

I can still see the puzzled expression on the face of the Roman Catholic priest who asked me to pray with him after I had addressed a meeting in Cork. As we sat down together he looked across at me and said: 'I'm really amazed that I'm sitting here asking you to pray with me. Before to-day I would not have even accepted the validity of your ordination.'

In Rome this year at the International Conference of the Catholic Charismatic renewal I listened to the witness of a Bishop from South America who testified to the revolution which had been wrought in his life after he was baptized in the Holy Spirit in his own Chapel. It had happened after reading a number of books by Protestant authors!

The witness of Dr. Vinson Synan, General Secretary of the Pentecostal Holiness Church, one of the oldest Pentecostal denominations and a historian of the revolution which the Holy Spirit has wrought in the minds and hearts of many, is of particular interest. After speaking about his upbringing in the narrow confines of the Pentecostal Holiness Church he goes on to say:

> The neo-pentecostal movement among Episcopalians, Lutherans, etc., had been difficult enough to accept—but the very idea of Catholics being baptized with the Holy Spirit was almost impossible to imagine. Growing up in Virginia, I had known Greek Orthodox and Roman Catholic churches across town and had learned to fear them. There was a world of difference, I felt, between our family's little wooden-framed Pentecostal Holiness church and the Catholic church downtown. The theological, social, and ecclesiastical chasm seemed too wide for the two to ever meet. After reading Paul Blanchard's 'American Freedom and Catholic Power', I felt that Catholicism was a greater threat to our American liberties than Communism.

Dr. Synan goes on to explain how in 1972 he accepted an invitation to speak at the Sixth International Conference on the Charismatic Renewal in the Roman Catholic Church. He described the scene as ten thousand, young and old from all walks of life gathered for a weekend of praise and prayer.

> I was overwhelmed with the atmosphere of love and spiritual excitement that hovered over the entire campus that weekend. My two roommates were college students—one Presbyterian and the other Catholic. They spent most of their time helping others pray for baptism in the Holy Spirit. Throughout the night one could hear the sounds of praise as groups in the various dormitories engaged in all-night prayer meetings. It was not unusual at any hour to hear groups walking across the campus shouting praises to God. The universal greeting was 'Praise the Lord' and 'Hallelujah'. During the day it was not unusual to see a priest or a layman laying hands on people praying for their baptism in the Spirit, for healing, or for deliverance from sin. It gradually dawned on me that I was seeing a Catholic-pentecostal 'camp meeting' right in the heartland of American Roman Catholicism—Notre Dame University!

> The Lord did a mighty work in my heart that week that has continued to this day. For the first time in my life, I found myself praying and worshipping with people against whom I had once harboured much prejudice and suspicion. I began to see these bible-carrying, scripture-quoting, Christ-exalting Catholic pentecostals as brothers and sisters in Christ. I came to have a greater appreciation for their staunch adherence

to the great fundamentals of the Christian faith, such as the Virgin Birth of Christ, the inspiration of the Scripture, the Deity, death and resurrection of Christ, etc. Their historic stand against divorce and abortion in favour of the sanctity of the home came into sharper focus.

Barriers to fellowship were broken down and walls of illwill and prejudice crumbled in a mighty sweep of love through the power of the Holy Spirit. I felt that surely we pentecostals had come to the Kingdom for such a time as this! [3]

In the renewal of the Holy Spirit which has swept over Ireland during the past three years we have seen many evidences of the power of God's Spirit to break through the most difficult barriers which history has erected.

It was Bishop Lesslie Newbigin over twenty years ago who urged in his book 'The Household of God' that we would only be able to present a full Christian message to the world when the Catholic and Reformed traditions were infused with the Pentecostal.

The decades which have witnessed the rise of the ecumenical movement have witnessed also the rise of innumerable bodies which, claiming exclusive possession of the Holy Spirit, have separated themselves from their fellow Christians. The growth of real charity between the great confessions which form the main body of Christians has been matched by the growth of an increasingly malicious and violent campaign of abuse from those movements on the flank. The propaganda of these organisations against the ecumenical movement is marked in many cases by such a blatant self-righteousness, and such a total negation of all charity, that one is tempted to despair of them altogether. But we must not yield to this temptation, for within these same movements we must recognize authentic marks of the Holy Spirit's presence, and also a witness to truth which the traditional Protestant and Catholic alike need to learn. . . We must ask them to consider whether by denying all fellowship with us, they do not sin against the Holy Spirit who is in them, and whether faithfulness to their Lord and ours does not absolutely require us to seek unity with one another.

And at the same time we must be willing to learn. In recent discussions of the Catholic-Protestant issue, and of the deadlock in which these discussions seem to have become immobilised, it is often suggested that the way forward may be found in a new understanding of the doctrine of the Holy Spirit. *But of course the illumination which is needed will never come as a result of purely academic theological study. May it not be that the great Churches of the Catholic and Protestant traditions will have to be humble enough to receive it in fellowship with their brethren in the various groups of the Pentecostal type with whom at present they have scarcely any Christian fellowship at all? The gulf which at present divides these groups from the ecumenical movement is the symptom of a real defect on both sides, and perhaps a resolute effort to bridge it is the next condition for further advance.*

These were prophetic words written by a man who spent most of his life working in a missionary situation in India and who saw the worst effects of the scandal of our dis-unity.

In the renewal which God is effecting by His Spirit all over the world today I see a fulfilment of those prophetic words. In our Lord's high priestly prayer in Saint John 17 He not only prayed that we might be one but also that 'we might become perfectly one'. The literal translation of the Greek is 'that they may be perfected into one' or 'that they may become full grown into one'. How are we to move towards that maturity in unity for which our blessed Lord prays. Surely it is only as we are together led by the Holy Spirit who is the Spirit of love, truth and unity.

We have already looked at the characteristic features of the charismatic renewal. There are several of those features which are particularly relevant to our thinking about the unity which the Holy Spirit is bringing.

The centrality and uniqueness of Jesus Christ

A basic mark of the Charismatic renewal is the centrality which is given to Jesus Christ. In the charismatic prayer meeting Christ is proclaimed as Lord and Saviour in word and song. In the very considerable proliferation of new songs that have accompanied the renewal a large number of these are taken up with the Biblical themes of the Lordship of Christ, His power to save and heal and sanctify. The Lord promised that when the Holy Spirit comes 'He will glorify me, for He will take what is mine and declare it to you'. 'The Counsellor, the Holy Spirit whom the Father will send in my Name, he will teach you all things and bring to your remembrance all that I have said to you.'

Saint John 14 v. 26

In writing to the Christians at Corinth Saint Paul was at pains to help them to discover what was truly of God in the religious experience which they had.

> You know that when you were heathen, you were led astray to dumb idols, however you may have been moved. Therefore I want you to

understand that no one speaking by the Spirit of God ever says 'Jesus be cursed!' and no one can say 'Jesus is Lord' except by the Holy Spirit.

1 Corinthians 12 vs. 2-3

The theme of the first National Conference of the Charismatic Renewal in Dublin was 'Jesus Christ is Lord'. In one of the major addresses on that theme Bishop Joseph McKinney a leader in the Charismatic Renewal in the United States declared: 'We come directly to the Father through the Son. I appreciate the difficulty which my Protestant brethren have with us Catholics if we insist on making the Virgin Mary the fourth person of the blessed Trinity'. At the International Conference in Rome in 1974 during the final Eucharist in Saint Peter's Basilica Cardinal Suenens declared: 'The only *real* person here today is Jesus', and when the Pope arrived to address that audience of 10,000 from many nations they were singing with arms upraised in worship: 'Alleluia, Jesus is Lord'. Surely here is the foundation stone for any real re-union of Christendom that we acknowledge with all our being, heart as well as head: "That Jesus Christ is Lord."

Archbishop Ramsey was surely right when he said:
Genuine renewal 'in Christ' brings closer together those who know themselves to be 'in Christ'. Here we find a new way of looking at the problems of unity. In dialogue between Churches we find ourselves asking, not, How can we unite our ecclesiastical structures just as we now find them? but rather, How can our church life be renewed, re-formed, or brought more effectively into the obedience of Christ . . . . Nothing is more heartening than to see Roman Catholics, Anglicans, and Christians of other communions sharing retreats together and asking together,

How can my own Church become more Christ like?[5]

Archbishop Ramsey was here saying in other words what his great predecessor William Temple had once said: 'The way to the union of Christendom does not lie through Committee rooms, though there is a task of formulation to be done there. It lies through personal union with the Lord so deep and real as to be comparable with His union with the Father.'[6] This is a truth which must never be lost sight of in our quest for unity and it is a message which the Holy Spirit is driving home with renewed force across the world today.

Openness to the direction of the Holy Spirit and expectant prayer

In a very real sense the Church was born out of the experience of Pentecost. The reception of the Holy Spirit by the early Christians was no unexpected 'bolt from the blue' which came upon them without warning. Saint Peter in his Pentecost sermon in Acts 2 was careful to point out to all the curious enquirers that what had happened to him and the others was simply what had been promised in the Scriptures, reiterated by the Lord and now made a reality by the infilling of the Holy Spirit in power.

Before His Ascension the risen Christ had told His disciples not to depart from Jerusalem but to wait for the promise of the Father, which he said 'You heard from me for John baptized with water, but before many days you shall be baptized with the Holy Spirit.'

Acts 1 vs. 4 and 5

The disciples had waited in expectant, believing prayer together, with one accord, in one place and the glorious promise was fulfilled 'They were all filled with the Holy Spirit and began to speak in other tongues as the Spirit gave them utterance.'

118

The Christian Church which is born in the power of the Holy Spirit can only continue its life in that same power. Too often we have acted as if the Church was our creation, operating under our control and our power and that is why we so often end up with so much confusion. Any working towards re-union that is not under the direction of the Holy Spirit is doomed to failure. Too often our Church meetings are begun with a vague prayer for guidance and we proceed to go through the agenda 'on our own steam' using our human resources and ingenuity. It is very significant that in the letters to the Churches in the Book of the Revelation each letter ends with the words 'He who has an ear let him hear what the Spirit says to the Churches'.

In all our 'conversations' about re-union how much time are we spending in listening together to what the Holy Spirit is saying to us? I am quite sure that we shall never make any significant advance in the realm of Christian unity until we take this matter much more seriously at every level of our Church life. Can we hear the Lord speaking above the noise of our learned discourses and our reasoned argument? How shall we hear if we do not listen? The renewal which the Holy Spirit is bringing is restoring to us the art of listening to Him expectantly.

If we do not listen to the Spirit our contribution will nearly always be along the lines of precedent, we shall argue from what has been and will almost certainly miss the new insights which the Lord longs to bring to us if only we will allow Him. I remember in one of the weekends of prayer together when Roman Catholics and Protestants were drawn together from all parts of Ireland a very powerful message in tongues was spoken. Its interpretation was to the effect: 'When I hung on the Cross I prayed 'Father forgive them for they do not know what they are doing—but you do know what you are doing and you are crucifying me afresh.'

Cardinal Bea once said: 'We go through the door of unity on our knees'. We can never hate those with whom we pray and the Lord is revealing a whole new dimension of co-existence when we learn to wait together in His presence. Even though a word may never be spoken, to be there in the presence of the Living Christ can take us far beyond our human resources however brilliant they may be. Cardinal Suenens in his book 'A New Pentecost' refers to the new dimensions which were opened to him in this expectant prayer:

> Prayer together, in which we open ourselves to the action of the Holy Spirit, is an ecumenical priority. This communal prayer to the Lord will confer on theological research which is indispensable, not just new energy but a new depth. And this prayer must not only introduce our work together, it should be part of the rhythm of our sessions, and would transform the whole atmosphere. Recently, I was present at some 'planning' sessions during meetings of leaders in the Charismatic Renewal. These sessions not only opened with a long period of spontaneous prayer, but were interspersed with prayer on the invitations of the president, to ask the Lord to send His Spirit to enlighten us on the subject under discussion and the decisions to be made. Prayer and work were organically bound together in the meeting itself, and one sensed a moving atmosphere of trust and humility before the Lord. If only the Holy Spirit would preside in the same way at our ecumenical dialogues . . . and at others!

He adds, with a certain wistfulness I'm sure:

Would it not be wonderful, too, if there were more interchange of this kind between Church leaders, at diocesan and parochial levels, and that this were a means of bringing together Christians in a common prayer, nourished by the word of God? The Acts of the Apostles tell us that when Peter was in prison the whole Christian community 'prayed to God for him unremittingly' (Acts 12 v. 5). Our prayer for the restoration of unity must be no less continuous, not only because this is our first step on the way of unity, but also because prayer is the indispensable climate that opens our hearts to its realisation.[7]

I have often longed at Church gatherings, Synods and Councils, when we are debating questions relating to our faith as if we were in a debating chamber, to stand up and just ask the whole audience to stop and spend an hour together in prayer before we proceed. I have often wondered what would happen if one had the courage to do that! In this expectant prayer which was the constant background music in the life of the early Church God was able to break in and reveal himself in the most remarkable and often disturbing ways. He was able to lead the Church from being simple 'prisoners to precedent' into men and women who followed him out into the dangerous open spaces. Even prison doors were opened in response to this expectant prayer and the impossible became gloriously possible. We need to be reassured that this will happen again today. In some wonderful ways this has been our experience since we came to establish the Centre for Christian renewal in Ireland. When the vision for such a Centre first came to us we prayed a lot about it and others joined us in prayer. Step by step the Lord opened the way often through very unusual circumstances and pointed to the next step. In the summer of

1973 while the vision was forming in my mind I was present at an inter-Church Leaders Conference of the Charismatic Renewal near Frankfurt in West Germany. Present at that Conference for one evening was Dr. Vinson Synan from the United States. At the end of the meeting on the first evening he stood up and said that he had come not intending to speak but the Lord was laying it strongly on his heart to read Isaiah 55 and he prayed that it would have a message for someone present. It was that reading which confirmed the vision which God had given us and at that time I had no idea that the location of the Christian Renewal Centre would be at the foothills of the tree-clad mountains of Mourne.

> For you shall go out in joy and be led forth in peace; the mountains and the hills before you shall break forth into singing and all the trees of the field shall clap their hands.
>
> Isaiah 55 v. 12

I have spoken about 'Vision'. It is a word which scares many people conveying as it often does weird associations with magic or ecstacy. But it is a thoroughly Biblical word. 'Where there is no vision the people perish.' Frequently it was through visions or pictures in the mind inspired by the Holy Spirit that men and women have been able to move forward to do great things for God.

One of the many 'visions' in the New Testament has a great deal to teach us today on this important matter of the reconciliation of Christians with one another as brothers in Christ. The vision came to no less a person than Saint Peter, a down to earth, matter of fact man if ever there was one. Through the vision which God gave to Peter there came one of the great advances in Christian history, the full acceptance of Gentiles into the Christian Church, a step so revolutionary that it makes our re-union schemes seem very tame in comparison.

In Acts 10 we read the story of how Peter saw the vision of the sheet let down from heaven.

> In it were all kinds of animals and reptiles and birds of the air. And there came a voice to him. 'Rise, Peter; kill and eat.' But Peter said, 'No, Lord; for I have never eaten anything that is common or unclean.' And the voice came to him again a second time, 'What God has cleansed, you must not call common.' This happened three times, and the thing was taken up at once to heaven.

Acts 10 vs. 12-16

As the full import of what was involved hit Peter, the 'reluctant missionary to the Gentiles', he obeyed the prompting of the Spirit and went to address an expectant congregation in the house of Cornelius. We can just see him as he entered the house of Cornelius, feeling somewhat as a Roman Catholic feels the first time he enters a Methodist Church or as a Protestant feels the first time he goes through the doors of a Roman Catholic monastery or convent. 'Truly I perceive', he said 'that God shows no partiality, but in every nation any one who fears him and does what is right is acceptable to him.' Then as he proceeded to speak about Jesus and the resurrection an amazing thing happened which utterly stunned Peter and his Jewish friends who accompanied him: 'While Peter was still saying this the Holy Spirit fell on all who heard the word'. Peter and the others had to believe the evidence of their eyes that God was truly no respector of persons. What he had reluctantly begun to accept with his mind he now had to accept with all his being. Then when he returned to Jerusalem the expected happened and it still happens today—'the circumcision party criticized him saying, Why did you go to uncircumcised men and eat with them?' Peter was on the mat! But there was no way

123

out. Something had happened that he could not deny. 'If God gave the same gift to them as He gave to us when we believed in the Lord Jesus Christ who was I that I could withstand God?' And to their credit 'When they heard this they were silenced. And they glorified God saying, 'Then to the Gentiles also God has granted repentance unto life.'

Acts 11 vs. 17 and 18

The feelings which Peter must have experienced have become very familiar to those of us especially in Ireland who have been involved in the 'ecumenism of the Spirit'. Recently when some of us were conducting a Day of Renewal in a midland town in Ireland where the majority of those attending were Roman Catholics, one Catholic layman said to me: 'You know many of our Catholic friends are saying to us: 'You are all becoming Protestant' and I replied 'And what do you think our Protestant friends are saying about us?' What a sense of humour God has! How traumatic such an experience can be was well illustrated at that same day of renewal by a Methodist layman who was present. He had been brought up in the North of Ireland where the Roman Catholics and Protestants had never worshipped together. He told me that in his first few meetings in the local convent where the prayer group met he had literally had a constant pain deep down in his stomach. 'Now,' he said, 'I know what real fellowship is.'

What followed Peter's vision and the breakthrough that came as a result of his ministry to the Gentiles led to one of the most important decisions taken by the early Church. At the Council of Jerusalem the Gentiles were accepted into the fellowship of the Christian Church. The letter which went from that assembly to the Gentiles is so obviously inspired by the Holy Spirit:

The brethren, both the apostles and the elders,

to the brethren who are of the Gentiles in Antioch and Syria and Cilicia, greeting. Since we have heard that some persons from us have troubled you with words, unsettling your minds, although we gave them no instructions, it has seemed good to us, having come to one accord, to choose men and send them to you with our beloved Barnabas and Paul, men who have risked their lives for the sake of our Lord Jesus Christ. We have therefore sent Judas and Silas, who themselves will tell you the same things by word of mouth. For it has seemed good to the Holy Spirit and to us to lay upon you no greater burden than these necessary things: that you abstain from what has been sacrificed to idols and from blood and from what is strangled and from unchastity. If you keep yourselves from these, you will do well. Farewell.

Acts 15 vs. 23-29

I like the priority which they recorded in that letter. 'It seemed good to the Holy Spirit and to us.' Perhaps like me you have often wondered why God chose a vision as the vehicle by which he led Peter to open his heart and his hands in brotherhood to the Gentiles. May it not have been that theological arguments or human reasoning would not have been sufficient to break down the prejudice which was in his bloodstream. And may it not be that God has to use similar means today to allow his Holy Spirit to reveal what it is He is asking of us? It is interesting to note that is not the end of the story for Peter. The prejudice towards the Gentiles and the fear of his fellow Jews was to cause him further embarrassment. Saint Paul tells us in his letter to the Galatians how he had to rebuke him for his hypocrisy:

But when Cephas came to Antioch I opposed him to his face, because he stood condemned.

125

For before certain men came from James, he ate with the Gentiles; but when they came he drew back and separated himself, fearing the circumcision party. And with him the rest of the Jews acted insincerely, so that even Barnabas was carried away by their insincerity. But when I saw that they were not straightforward about the truth of the gospel, I said to Cephas before them all, 'If you, though a Jew live like a Gentile and not like a Jew, how can you compel the Gentiles to live like Jews?'

Galatians 2 vs. 11-14

The temptation is always there to 'draw back' fearing whatever party criticizes us. 'You've really been going too far, old boy.' 'You are confusing the issue for so many people. You are rocking the boat with all this talk about us being fellow-heirs together in the family of Christ.'

Even in the warm fellowship which many have experienced in the Charismatic renewal there is the temptation to draw back when the cold wind of criticism blows or the subtle finger of fear is pointing our way.

Stephen Clark, one of the young leaders in the Roman Catholic Church Renewal in the United States pointed out the real danger of introversion among Roman Catholics who have received so much from other traditions in the renewal of the Spirit. Writing in New Covenant magazine he had this to say:

There is a tendency among Catholics to be baptized in the Spirit and then withdraw into their own all-Catholic groups and go on from there. As a result, many Catholics in the charismatic renewal in the United States only go part way. They are baptized in the Spirit and may begin to open up to tongues and prophecy (although

126

ing in the Eucharist the reality which they cannot deny—their deep unity in the Spirit of Christ. It seems to me that so long as any Church persists in fencing the Lord's Table in and making it their own we will not see a real way forward. It is the Lord's Table for the people who love the Lord at the feast which He provides for all who love Him in sincerity and truth. It may be that the first step in the road to inter-communion will be asking God's forgiveness for the great damage we have done in failing 'to discern the Lord's body'. Must we wait until a group of theologians tell us it is legitimate to do that which in our hearts we know is real already in our experience?

In that same Chapter in Ephesians Saint Paul goes on to speak of the road we are travelling on 'till we all attain to the unity of the faith and of the knowledge of the Son of God, to mature manhood to the measure of the stature of the fullness of Christ'. Then he goes on to enunciate the important principle which must always govern our approach to one another in the body of Christ:

> Speaking the truth in love we are to grow up in every way into Him who is the head even Christ, from whom the whole body, joined and knit together by every joint with which it is supplied, when each part is working properly, makes bodily growth and upbuilds itself in love.
>
> Ephesians 4 vs. 15 and 16

At the Fourth Assembly of the World Council of Churches held at Uppsala in 1968 Father Robert Tucci, S.J. gave an address on 'The Ecumenical Movement and the Roman Catholic Church'. 'The Centre of the ecumenical movement', he said, 'can only be Christ Himself who, through the action of his Spirit, is drawing us all by the way of repentance towards the fullness of unity. For us Roman Catholics also, the union of all Christians in the one Church of Christ cannot be the victory of one

Church over another, but the victory of Christ over our divisions, our conversion to Christ in which we are loyal to the promptings of the Holy Spirit which is the Spirit of Unity, and which can lead us along ways that we cannot today foresee.' Cardinal Suenens was surely right when he said at the Second National Conference of the Charismatic Renewal in Ireland. 'I believe that the solution of disunity will not finally be the result of a dialogue between the Church of Rome and the Church of Canterbury or the Church of Moscow. It will not be a dialogue between the Churches as such but a dialogue between Rome and Jesus, Canterbury and Jesus, Moscow and Jesus so that we can become more and more united in Him. 'Let us come back home', he said, 'and home means the Upper Room at Pentecost.'

To come back there will mean a revolution not only in our individual lives but in our Churches as well. It was in the Upper Room that the disciples were gathered in prayer with one accord when the mighty power of God's Spirit broke into their lives and disturbed their whole way of life. Those who have been there cannot but speak the things they have seen and heard. Those who have been to 'the house of Cornelius' and witnessed the Spirit of God being poured out in refreshing power upon those of a different tradition cannot go back to their sectarian ghettoes.

At the Second Irish National Conference of the Charismatic Renewal we had the most representative gathering of Christians ever held in Ireland. Almost 4,000 from many different traditions were together for an unforgettable weekend of prayer and praise. With a choir of eighty young people from Belfast I had the privilege of leading a festival of praise on the second evening of the Conference. I shall never forget that scene as from every corner of Ireland we joined hands to sing in unison.

Bind us together Lord, bind us together
With cords that cannot be broken;
Bind us together Lord, bind us together,
Bind us together in Love.
There is only one God, there is only one King,
There is only one Body, that is why I sing.
Fit for the glory of God, purchased by His
precious Son.
Born with the right to be clean, for Jesus the
victory has won.
You are the family of God, you are the promise
divine,
You are God's chosen desire, you are the
glorious new wine. [10]

From the platform one could clearly discern the shape of a cross unconsciously cast by the arc lights for the film cameras. It reminded me of a vision that had been shared at a Conference two years earlier. It was a choir of people marching through the country from North to South carrying the cross. As they moved across the country apparently lifeless bodies came to life and joined the chorus of praise as the vast concourse moved in joyful praise to God. The word that was read from Isaiah 43 had a real significance for us all that evening.

> Remember not the former things, nor consider the things of old. Behold I am doing a new thing; now it springs forth, do you not perceive it? I will make a way in the wilderness and rivers in the desert. The wild beasts will honour me, the jackals and the ostriches; for I give water in the wilderness, rivers in the desert, to give drink to my chosen people, the people whom I formed for myself that they might declare my praise.

> Isaiah 43 vs. 18-21

131

God is really doing a new thing in our day. By His Spirit He is calling us out beyond the frontiers, out of our 'safe corners' into a future that we do not yet see. He has the power to do what seems impossible 'to make a way in the wilderness' even through the unfriendly, stubborn undergrowth of our divisions and fears; even through the hard rocks of our prejudices and pre-conceived ideas. Out of the well-spring of the life of Christ bursts the streams through the dry deserts of our dying institutions. God's Spirit comes to baptize with power and with fire. The power of the Spirit comes to resurrect the Church from its sleep of death and fire of the Spirit to burn up all the dross. It is a painful process for the Church to know this purging and cleansing flame but it is essential if we are to witness to a living Saviour in a world that desperately needs to know that message. And there is so much that has to be burned up in all of our traditions. 'We would like to see Jesus' was the plea of the enquiring Greeks when they met the disciples. Sometimes unconsciously and more often today quite vocally the world is saying the same to the Christian Churches. All that obscures His face and clouds our vision of Him must go.

> Jesus is the answer for our world today
> Beside Him there's no other
> Jesus is the way.

For me one of the most challenging moments of the ninth International Conference of the Catholic Charismatic Renewal was in the Basilica of Saint Peter on Pentecost Monday when a very clear word of prophecy was spoken. I believe it was a word not only for those who were gathered there but for Christians all over the world.

> Because I love you, I want to show you what I am doing in the world today. I want to prepare you for what is to come. Days of darkness are coming on the world, days of tribulation . . .

132

Buildings that are now standing will not be standing. Supports that are there for my people now will not be there. I want you to be prepared, my people, to know only me and to cleave to me and to have me in a way deeper than ever before. I will lead you into the desert . . . I will strip you of everything that you are depending on now, so you depend just on me. A time of darkness is coming on the world, but a time of glory is coming for my church, a time of glory is coming for my people. I will pour out on you all the gifts of my Spirit. I will prepare you for spiritual combat; I will prepare you for a time of evangelism that the world has never seen . . . And when you have nothing but me, you will have everything: land, fields, homes, and brothers and sisters and love and joy and peace more than ever before. Be ready, my people, I want to prepare you . . .

. . . You have known the truth these days. You have experienced the truth these days. It is clear to you at this moment what the truth is. It is the truth of my kingdom, my kingdom that will prevail . . . I want you to take that truth, to rest in that truth, to believe in that truth, not to compromise it, not to lose it in confusion, not to be timid about it, but to stand simply, in love, but to stand simply, firmly rooted in the truth as foundation stones upon which my church can have new life and new power.

In prayer one day the Lord showed me a picture or a vision of what He is doing at this time in His Church all over the world. I found myself in a high watch-tower in the middle of a dense forest. All around the watch-tower were beautiful healthy green trees swaying in the sunshine in a warm breeze. Further off in the distance the forest had been burned clear and the fire continued to burn far into the distance. In the area that had been cleared fresh new trees were springing up to join those in the foreground. No workmen or machinery could be seen in the picture. What I felt God was trying to say was this. 'By the power of My Spirit I am purging and purifying my Church, preparing a people for my praise. I am burning up all the undergrowth and dead wood, all that prevents healthy growth and I am doing it by my Spirit—no man is doing this work.'

Behind the Christian Renewal Centre at Rostrevor the wooded slopes of the Mountains of Mourne reach down to the waters edge. From early spring to late Autumn those hillsides are a blaze of colour. The deciduous trees daily change their colours and the varied shades of evergreens command the upper slopes. For me it provides a vivid picture of what God is doing with His Church in the world today. He is not producing a dull monochrome. In that forest, part of His creation the varied trees offer Him their silent praise. He wants to reflect with even greater glory the infinite variety of His 'New Creation', the Church as He gathers a people for His praise out of 'every tongue and people and nation'.

May we move today towards a clearer understanding of that great vision of Saint John the Divine.

> Then he showed me the river of the water of life, bright as crystal, flowing from the throne of God and of the Lamb through the middle of the street of the city; also, on either side of the river, the tree of life with its twelve kinds of fruit, yielding its fruit each month; and the leaves of the tree were for the healing of the nations. There shall no more be anything accursed, but the throne of God and of the Lamb shall be in it, and his

servants shall worship him; they shall see his
face, and his name shall be on their foreheads.
And night shall be no more; they need no light
of lamp or sun, for the Lord God will be their
light, and they shall reign for ever and ever.

Revelation 22 vs. 1-5

(1) New Delhi Report, 1961. World Council of Churches.

(2) Report of the Faith and Order Commission of the British Council of Churches.

(3) *Charismatic Bridges* by Vinson Synan. Page 22 *Word of Life Books* 1975.

(4) *The Household of God* by Lesslie Newbigin. Page 109 S.C.M. 1947.

(5) *The Future of the Church*. Arthur Michael Ramsey and Leon-Joseph Suenens, S.C.M. Press 1971.

(6) Readings in St. John's Gospel, William Temple. Page ——, MacMillan & Co. 1961.

(7) *A New Pentecost?* Cardinal Suenens. Darton, Longman & Todd 1975.

(8) New Covenant.

(9) *The Future of the Church*. Ramsey & Suenens. Page 9, S.C.M. Press, 1971.

(10) *Bind us together*. Church Missionary Society.

For Your Meditation

So if there is any encouragement in Christ, any incentive of love, any participation in the Spirit, any affection and sympathy, complete my joy by being of the same mind, having the same love, being in full accord and of one mind. Do nothing from selfishness or conceit, but in humility count others better than yourselves. Let each of you look not only to his own interests, but also to the interests of others. Have this mind among yourselves, which is yours in Christ Jesus, who, though he was in the form of God, did not count equality with God a thing to be grasped, but emptied himself, taking the form of a servant, being born in the likeness of men. And being found in human form he humbled himself and became obedient unto death, even death on a cross. Therefore God has highly exalted him and bestowed on him the name which is above every name, that at the name of Jesus every knee should bow, in heaven and on earth and under the earth, and every tongue confess that Jesus Christ is Lord, to the glory of God the Father. Therefore, my beloved, as you have always obeyed, so now, not only as in my presence but much more in my absence, work out your own salvation with fear and trembling; for God is at work in you, both to will and to work for his good pleasure. Do all things without grumbling or questioning, that you may be blameless and innocent, children of God without blemish in the midst of a crooked and perverse generation, among whom you shine as lights in the world, holding fast the word of life, so that in the day of Christ I may be proud that I did not run in vain or labour in vain.

Philippians 2 vs. 1-16

A Prayer

I do not pray for these only, but also for those
who believe in me through their word, that they
may all be one; even as thou, Father, art in me,
and I in thee, that they also may be in us, so
that the world may believe that thou hast sent
me. The glory which thou hast given me I have
given to them, that they may be one even as we
are one, I in them and thou in me, that they may
become perfectly one, so that the world may
know that thou hast sent me and hast loved them
even as thou hast loved me. Father, I desire that
whom thou hast given me, they also, may be
with me where I am, to behold my glory which
thou hast given me in thy love for me before the
foundation of the world. O righteous Father, the
world has not known thee, but I have known
thee: and these know that thou hast sent me. I
made known to them thy name, and I will make
it known, that the love with which thou hast
loved me may be in them, and I in them.

John 17 vs. 20-26

A Prayer

And it is my prayer that your love may abound
more and more, with knowledge and all discern-
ment, so that you may approve what is excellent, and may be pure and blameless for the day
of Christ, filled with the fruits of righteousness
which come through Jesus Christ, to the glory
and praise of God.

Philippians 1 vs. 9-11

7. "Love One Another"

In the New Testament reconciliation goes to the heart of every relationship; it applies to every area of life where barriers may be erected both in our individual lives and in our relationships with others. 'Divide and conquer' is a favourite tactic of the devil. It is always his purpose to bring such division as will paralyse the witness of God's people and render the Church as ineffectual as possible. He does this as we have seen by subtle means on the national and international levels. He also attempts to do it on the local level and even on the family level with disastrous and sad results. And how many ways the devil can come into a local Church or fellowship to bring disputes and divisions, to take our eyes off Christ and His Kingdom into *our* efforts, *our* gifts, *our* Church.

This is no new phenomenon. It arose early in the life of the Christian Church and came so often along the lines of personality cults. In writing to the Christians in the Church in Corinth Paul had to deal firmly with those who were dividing up in camps and following favourite preachers or teachers.

> For it has been reported to me by Chloe's people that there is quarrelling among you, my brethren. What I mean is that each one of you says, 'I belong to Paul', or 'I belong to Apollos', or 'I

belong to Cephas', or 'I belong to Christ'. Is Christ divided? Was Paul crucified for you? Or were you baptized in the name of Paul? I am thankful that I baptized none of you except Crispus and Gaius; lest any one should say that you were baptized in my name.

I Corinthians 1 vs. 11-15

In my work I have the opportunity of visiting many different Churches and fellowships and one of the saddest things to see is the great division that so often exists between those who are meant to be one in the Spirit of Jesus worshipping together and meant to be working together. How it must grieve the heart of Christ to see His body so rent by internal strife, division and bitterness. I often ask how can God bless a Church or fellowship which is not living in the forgiveness and peace of Jesus Christ?

Before God can really bless our Churches and make them effective witnesses to Him there is much healing that needs to take place between individual members and this goes for relationships between clergy and leaders too. Envy and jealousy, pride and power seeking do not provide the soil in which the Holy Spirit can work to bring glory to Jesus.

Only as we live in mutual forgiveness and love can we grow in grace and really be effective. 'If we walk in the light as He is in the light we have fellowship with one another and the blood of Jesus Christ His Son cleanses us from all sin.' As Christ reminded us we cannot be agents of reconciliation if we are not being reconciled ourselves.

Or how can you say to your brother, 'Brother, let me take out the speck that is in your eye,' when you yourself do not see the log that is in your own eye? You hypocrite, first take the log

139

out of your own eye, and then you will see
clearly to take out the speck that is in your
brother's eye.

Saint Luke 6 v. 42

This is a hard lesson to learn and one which we constantly have to go on learning.

It is surely very significant that in the solemn meeting which our Lord had with the disciples in the upper room before His crucifixion again and again He appealed to them 'to love one another'. 'A new commandment I give you that you love one another as I have loved you.'

The most powerful acted parable which the Lord left with His disciples was when He took a towel and basin and went around to wash the disciples' feet. Having washed their feet He went back to His place and explained to them:

> Do you know what I have done to you? You
> call me Teacher and Lord; and you are right,
> for so I am. If I then, your Lord and Teacher,
> have washed your feet, you also ought to wash
> one another's feet. For I have given you an
> example, that you also should do as I have done
> to you. Truly, truly, I say to you, a servant is
> not greater than his master; nor is he who is
> sent greater than he who sent him. If you know
> these things, blessed are you if you do them.

Saint John 13 vs. 12b-17

'By this shall all men know that you are my disciples if you have love for one another.' This is the real test of Christian life. The Lord did not say: 'By your doctrine, your creeds, your rituals, your ceremonies—however important these may be—but by the love you have for one another'. And this is no sentimental soppy love—it is *agape*—a caring, suffering love which lays down its life for the brothers.

> This is my commandment, that you love one
> another as I have loved you. Greater love has no
> man than this, that a man lay down his life for
> his friends. You are my friends if you do what
> I command you. No longer do I call you ser-
> vants, for the servant does not know what his
> master is doing; but I have called you friends,
> for all that I have heard from my Father I have
> made known to you. You did not choose me,
> but I chose you and appointed you that you
> should go and bear fruit and that your fruit
> should abide; so that whatever you ask the
> Father in my name, he may give it to you. This
> I command you, to love one another.
>
> Saint John 15 vs. 12-17

It is to this love that the Lord is calling His Church
today in every expression of its life and by the Holy Spirit
He is pouring that love into our hearts for it is a super-
natural love. Naturally we could never love like that. I
find it very moving that one of the most beautiful writings
on Christian love in this practical way in the New Testament was penned by Saint John in his first Epistle and he
was the one who once wanted to burn up in anger a village that would not receive Christ. Here is what he wrote
in 1 John: 4.

> Beloved, let us love one another; for love is of
> God, and he who loves is born of God and
> knows God. He who does not love does not know
> God; for God is love. In this the love of God
> was made manifest among us, that God sent his
> only Son into the world, so that we might live
> through Him. In this is love, not that we loved
> God but that He loved us and sent His Son to be
> the expiation for our sins. Beloved, if God so
> loved us, we also ought to love one another. No

man has ever seen God; if we love one another, God abides in us and his love is perfected in us. There is no fear in love, but perfect love casts out fear. For fear has to do with punishment, and he who fears is not perfected in love. We love, because He first loved us. If any one says, 'I love God', and hates his brother, he is a liar; for he who does not love his brother whom he has seen, cannot love God whom he has not seen. And this commandment we have from him, that he who loves God should love his brother also.

1 John 4 vs. 7-12 and 18-21

It was a pagan historian of the first century who observed of the early Church 'SEE HOW THESE CHRISTIANS LOVE ONE ANOTHER' and it is that love expressed not only within the Christian fellowship but extended out into the world that is still the greatest example to the world that there is a God who cares.

It is in fellowships and Churches that have experienced a deep renewal of the graces and gifts of the Holy Spirit that this is being manifest in a living way today. As men and women experience the great grace and love of Christ they are being led out to share that love with others.

Freely, freely you have received
Freely, freely give.

I saw this demonstrated in a remarkable way in the life of the Church of the Redeemer in Houston, Texas, a Church I visited several years ago. It was a downtown Church that years ago was attended by large congregations but now found itself almost an island in the midst of a completely new situation. Into the once large houses that had been rich suburbia had moved thousands of immigrants. Filled with the Spirit and open to His leading the Rector and a small group of Christians there were led to see a total transformation of the life of the parish. They found a new depth of commitment to Jesus Christ, a new reality in worship, a new joy in living. A costly joy which led them to share their homes with all kinds of inadequate people, drug addicts, alcoholics, people whose marriages had broken. These people were brought into a loving fellowship where real healing of mind and body took place. It was at once a reminder to me that true reconciliation is always by way of the Cross via the incarnation. Such love is costly. It costs everything and Christ gave all.

In our shattered and broken society the world needs to see again a demonstration of the caring, sacrificial love of Christ manifest through the Christian body. The world will quite rightly pass by a Church which fails to practise what it preaches. To the wrangling members of the Christian Churches in Galatia Saint Paul had a warning which is true in every age 'If you bite and devour one another take heed that you are not consumed by one another'.

We have already noted one of the most remarkable features of the renewal which the Holy Spirit is bringing to the Church today is the new awareness of the meaning of the 'body of Christ'. This term, so central to Saint Paul's teaching about the Church has remained for many just another pleasant theological concept carrying a kind of mystical aura far removed from the reality of life on the High Street. Today God is making this great truth a reality in the lives of many more people. The theme of reconciliation is central to its practical outworking, for it has to do with our relationship with one another.

In 1 Corinthians v. 12 Saint Paul gives some very clear teaching about the nature of the body of Christ and our relationship to one another within it:

For just as the body is one and has many members and all the members of the body, though many, are one body, so it is with Christ. For by one Spirit we were all baptized into one body—Jews or Greeks, slaves or free—and all were made to drink of one Spirit.

But God has so adjusted the body, giving the greater honour to the inferior part, that there may be no discord in the body, but that the members may have the same care for one another. If one member suffers, all suffer together; if one member is honoured, all rejoice together. Now you are the body of Christ and individually members of it.

1 Corinthians 12 vs. 12 and 13, 24B-27

This togetherness in the body of Christ can only be sustained by the power of the Spirit working in our lives together and it demands the fruit of the Spirit to maintain it—'love, joy, peace, patience, kindness, goodness, faithfulness, gentleness, and self-control'.

Galatians 5 vs. 22 and 23

The analogy of the 'body' is such a powerful one for the understanding of our mutual inter-dependance within the Church. Each one needs the other and feels the other's pain and there is no useless member in 'the body of Christ'. Saint Paul goes so far in 1 Corinthians v. 11 to say that spiritual weakness and even spiritual death are a consequence of 'not discerning the Lord's body'. If I am in a wrong relationship with another member of the Church the vital lifeblood of the body of Christ is prevented from flowing through every member and the quicker it is put right the sooner the body will regain life and health.

It is Saint Paul's prayer for the Christians in Rome that:

The God of steadfastness and encouragement may grant you to live in such harmony with one another, in accord with Christ Jesus, that together you may with one voice glorify the God and Father of our Lord Jesus Christ.

Romans 15 vs. 5-6

The beautiful hymn of the Wesleyan revival captures so well the enduring truth of mutual love which is at the heart of Christian fellowship.

All praise to our redeeming Lord,
Who joins us by His grace,
And bids us, each to each restored,
Together seek His face.
He bids us build each other up;
And, gathered into one,
To our high calling's glorious hope
We hand in hand go on.
The gift which He on one bestows,
We all delight to prove;
The grace through every vessel flows,
In purest streams of love.
Even now we think and speak the same,
And cordially agree;
Concentred all, through Jesu's name,
In perfect harmony.
We all partake the joy of one,
The common peace we feel,
A peace to sensual minds unknown,
A joy unspeakable.
And if our fellowship below
In Jesus be so sweet,
What heights of rapture shall we know
When round His throne we meet![1]

In reading that lovely book by Bishop J. V. Taylor 'The Go-between God' my attention was drawn to the

145

little Greek word that has great importance. It is the word ALLELON and means 'each other' or 'one another'. Bishop Taylor says it is a word which rings like a clarion bell throughout the New Testament. I have found it a rich exercise to take a concordance and follow that little word throughout the pages of the New Testament. I am quite sure that if every Church was to do a thorough study of that little word as it occurs in the Bible we would have a transformation of our life together. I have referred already to the important words of our Lord in the Upper Room that we should 'love one another'. We are 'to forbear with one another and to forgive one another'. (Colossians 3 v. 13). We are 'to bear one another's burdens and so fulfil the law of Christ' (Galatians 6 v. 2). We are 'to serve one another' (Galatians 5 v. 13). We are 'to welcome one another as Christ has welcomed us' (Romans 15 v. 7). We are 'to be subject one to another out of reverence for Christ' (Ephesians 5 v. 21). We are 'to greet one another with a holy kiss' (Romans 16 v. 16, 1 Peter 5 v. 14).

And Saint James reminds us of how the tongue is to be bridled so that this mutual love might be maintained. How much harm and suffering, sin and evil could be averted if we would follow his simple advice. 'Do not speak evil against one another brethren' (James 4 v. 11). 'Do not grumble brethren, against one another, that you may not be judged' (James 5 v. 9). 'Therefore confess your sins to one another, and pray for one another that you may be healed' (James 5 v. 16).

It is surely very significant that when the Lord appeared to the disciples after the resurrection as recorded in Saint John 20 the first words He spoke were about peace and forgiveness.

> Jesus said to them again, 'Peace be with you. As the Father has sent me, even so I send you.' And when he had said this, he breathed on them, and

said to them, 'Receive the Holy Spirit. If you forgive the sins of any, they are forgiven; if you retain the sins of any, they are retained.'

John 20 vs. 21-23

This principle of forgiveness enshrined in the words of the Lord's Prayer 'forgive us our trespasses as we forgive those who trespass against us' operates in every sphere of human relationships. How many relationships both in the Church and outside it are ruined because of lack of forgiveness. When I refuse to forgive someone who has wronged me I allow a root of bitterness to grow in me which may manifest itself in all kinds of mental and physical hurt. Indeed I have known people who have suffered severe physical disability through not having forgiven or been forgiven. God knows and grieves over the ways in which we hurt each other in so many ways. Very often in my experience as a marriage counsellor I have met a couple whose marriage has become so sour that love has turned to hate. Almost always it has begun with something fairly small and to the outsider apparently trivial. Because it has been allowed to go unhealed and unforgiven it has grown into a festering sore that is almost impossible to heal. Isn't this so often the case in the Church too. A little division occurs which if not dealt with in time becomes something really hurtful and makes the Church's witness ineffectual and brings shame on the name of Christ.

I'm sure we often quote the beautiful promise of our Lord given in Saint Matthew 18 'Where two or three are gathered together in my Name there am I in the midst of them'.

It is very important, however, to read those words in the context in which Jesus spoke about any dispute that may arise between members of the Church. Have you

147

ever in your Church fellowship seen this principle applied which our Lord Himself enunciated?

> If your brother sins against you, go and tell him his fault, between you and him alone. If he listens to you, you have gained your brother. But if he does not listen, take one or two others along with you, that every word may be confirmed by the evidence of two or three witnesses. If he refuses to listen to them, tell it to the Church; and if he refuses to listen even to the church, let him be to you as a Gentile and a tax collector. Truly, I say to you, whatever you bind on earth shall be bound in heaven, and whatever you loose on earth shall be loosed in heaven. Again I say to you, if two of you agree on earth about anything they ask, it will be done for them by my Father in heaven. For where two or three are gathered in my name, there am I in the midst of them.
>
> Saint Matthew 18 vs. 15-20

Earlier in the same Gospel in the Beatitudes our Lord had said something similar.

> So if you are offering your gift at the altar, and there remember that your brother has something against you, leave your gift there before the altar and go; first be reconciled to your brother, and then come and offer your gift.
>
> Saint Matthew 5 vs. 23 and 24

How much untold harm can be done within a local Church where these basic principles are ignored. If instead of going to the person who has wronged me I go off to someone else and speak about how hurt I am I only extend the hurtful cancer. If I can go in love and humility to him I may gain my brother. How often you find that your opinion of someone is so often coloured by someone else's prejudice because you have never taken the trouble to meet your brother or your sister face to face. In the beautiful letter which Saint Paul wrote to the Philippians so full of joy and thanksgiving there was just one fly in the ointment, two of the women had a disagreement that was harming the rest of the body. Lovingly Saint Paul addresses them by name at the end of the letter 'I beseech Euodia and I entreat Syntyche to agree in the Lord'.

How can the Church become a reconciling influence in society and the world if there are wounds and hurts in the body that have not been healed? If roots of bitterness are allowed to grow they prevent the healthy growth of the body and frustrate its outreach to a needy world. Earlier in the letter to the Philippians Saint Paul had said: 'Do all things without grumbling or questioning, that you may be blameless and innocent, children of God without blemish in the midst of a crooked and perverse generation among whom you shine as lights in the world.'
Philippians 2 vs. 14-15

How sad it is that the local Church which should be the place of healing is often the last place that people will go for help with problems that seem to overwhelm them. Early in my ministry I remember being greatly challenged when a doctor in the town where I worked said to me: 'You know that many of the patients who come to my surgery should really be going to you. Their problems are very often not physical but spiritual.' What a travesty of the 'body of Christ' it is in so many of our Churches when people come sometimes in desperate need and go out again without anyone taking any notice of them. The place that should be the 'family home' where the needs of the family are freely met by the other members becomes a stage where weekly charades are acted out by players pretending to be what they are not.

I sometimes feel that when we hand out service books at the back of the Church we also dispense invisible masks for people to wear so that their real selves might not be exposed. We so often suffer in Church from what a friend of mine has called 'ecclesiastical arthritis'. We even find it hard to smile.

If you have ever tried to introduce 'the kiss of peace' into a Church service even in the modified form of a handshake you will understand how traumatic that experience can be for some people.

One of the pre-requisites of renewal in the Church is a re-discovery of our togetherness. And when the Church becomes a place of healing we won't have to go out and persuade people to come in; our problem will be finding time to deal with all who want to come.

Charles Wesley expressed so well what I am trying to say in a hymn that we should use more often.

> Help us to help each other, Lord,
> Each other's cross to bear;
> Let each his friendly aid afford,
> And feel his brother's care.
> Touched by the loadstone of thy love,
> Let all our hearts agree;
> And ever toward each other move,
> And ever move toward thee.
> This is the bond of perfectness,
> Thy spotless charity;
> O let us still, we pray, possess
> The mind that was in thee.[2]

[1] *All Praise to Our Redeeming Lord*, Charles Wesley.

[2] *Help Us to Help Each Other, Lord*, Charles Wesley.

For Your Meditation

I appeal to you therefore, brethren, by the mercies of God, to present your bodies as a living sacrifice, holy and acceptable to God, which is your spiritual worship. Do not be conformed to this world but be transformed by the renewal of your mind, that you may prove what is the will of God, what is good and acceptable and perfect. For by the grace given to me I bid every one among you not to think of himself more highly than he ought to think, but to think with sober judgement, each according to the measure of faith which God has assigned him. For as in one body we have many members, and all the members do not have the same function, so we, though many, are one body in Christ, and individually members one of another. Having gifts that differ according to the grace given to us, let us use them: if prophecy, in proportion to our faith; if service, in our serving; he who teaches, in his teaching; he who exhorts, in his exhortation; he who contributes, in liberality; he who gives aid, with zeal; he who does acts of mercy, with cheerfulness. Let love be genuine; hate what is evil, hold fast to what is good; love one another with brotherly affection; outdo one another in showing honour. Never flag in zeal, be aglow with the Spirit, serve the Lord. Rejoice in your hope, be patient in tribulation, be constant in prayer. Contribute to the needs of the saints, practise hospitality.

Romans 12 vs. 1-13

A Prayer

May the God of steadfastness and encouragement grant you to live in such harmony with one another, in accord with Christ Jesus, that together you may with one voice glorify the God and Father of our Lord Jesus Christ.

Romans 15 vs. 5 and 6

8. Power To Love

When I pray 'Lord renew the Church' I must always go on to add 'and begin with me'. It is very easy to criticize the Church for its lack of spiritual power, for its dryness and its sterility. All along we have been stressing God's call and God's challenge to His people, how together we are to hear what the Spirit is saying and how together we can respond to that challenge and demonstrate His power and love in the world. That corporate response is necessary but it begins with a personal response. Christianity is not an individualistic faith but it is a deeply personal one. Many Christians who have been deeply sensitive to human need and concerned about their fellow man have tended to burn themselves up in a constant round of ceaseless activity. I know this can be so really true in the life of a clergyman.

At the heart of the renewal which the Holy Spirit is bringing to the Church to-day there is first a deep renewal of our individual lives when we discover again that the power by which we minister must be God's and not ours. It is very significant that in the account of creation in Genesis man's first full day in the world was a day of rest. Renewal begins with God, in the sanctuary, in the place of rest. It is only when God can bring me to that place of rest when I can hear Him that I can lay down my burdens and my concerns and receive from Him the almighty power He longs to share with me. It is not unusual for many people to come to a deep experience of God and to be 'baptized in the Spirit' when they have 'come to the end of themselves' and they feel completely drained of any resources to help themselves or others. It is tragically possible to be so busy for God that we never take time to hear what He is saying to us.

The questions we want to deal with here are simple and fundamental. How can I receive the promised power of God? How can I be baptized with the Holy Spirit and what effect will this have on my life?

In my contact with people and from my own experience I find that so many are in a similar position to the Christians whom Paul encountered at Ephesus who had 'never even heard that there was a Holy Spirit'. In so much traditional Church teaching the Holy Spirit has been the forgotten person of the blessed Trinity. With the translation of Spirit as Ghost in so many versions of the Bible and in our liturgies people could be excused for thinking of the Holy Spirit as some vague kind of influence that has little relevance to our everyday world. What a tragedy that there has been such a neglect of such a vital doctrine. Even those who have 'doctrinally' and 'theologically' taught about the Holy Spirit have seldom been encouraged to expect the Holy Spirit to work in power to-day. What we believe with our heads we need to experience in our hearts. We need what my friend, David du Plessis has called 'the eighteen inch drop'. It is this experience which has become a reality for so many and is transforming the life of the Church to-day in what has commonly been called the 'Charismatic renewal'.

Personally, as a minister in the Church of Ireland I had believed in the power of the Holy Spirit. I had often preached on the subject especially at Pentecost. I knew

I was a Christian. I had yielded my life to Christ in faith and I was trying to serve Him as a pastor. I was ordained for twelve years before I knew the experience of being baptized with the Holy Spirit. I know that this is a reflection on the unbelief of the Church to which I belong and the long neglect of a basic doctrine of our faith. The neglect of a living experience of the power of the Holy Spirit in the lives of individuals and Churches is I am convinced the greatest single factor in the failure of the Church to-day to be a powerful witness to Christ in an unbelieving world. In each of the four gospels it is recorded that John the Baptist promised that Christ will 'baptize with the Holy Spirit'. The Lord Himself in His charge to the disciples in the Upper Room promised that His Holy Spirit would come to dwell within them, to guide and teach and lead them.

After His resurrection when He appeared to the disciples to tell them about their future mission in His Name He left them in no doubt that it would not be with their human strength that they would undertake the task to which He had called them. Saint Luke records how He had set the challenge before them of bringing the good news of the Gospel to every nation. Then the Lord added:

> And behold I send the promise of my Father upon you; but stay in the city until you are clothed with power from on high.

> Saint Luke 24 v. 49

Again before His Ascension He repeated the warning:

> And while staying with them he charged them not to depart from Jerusalem, but to wait for the promise of the Father, which, he said, you heard from me, for John baptized with water, but before many days you shall be baptized with the Holy Spirit.

> But you shall receive power when the Holy

155

Spirit has come upon you; and you shall be my witnesses in Jerusalem and in all Judea and Samaria and to the end of the earth.

Acts 1 vs. 4, 5 and 8

Those disciples had already witnessed the resurrection. They had a message to tell the world. They were filled with joy that their Lord was alive. The Lord had breathed His Spirit within them. St. Luke tells us 'He had presented himself alive after His passion by many proofs, appearing to them during forty days and speaking of the kingdom of God'. Surely this was something to tell the world about. But no, the Lord repeated His warning that they were to wait until they received 'Power from on high'. They would be immersed in the Holy Spirit. Then on the day of Pentecost as they were all together in one place

> suddenly a sound came from heaven like the rush of a mighty wind, and it filled all the house where they were sitting. And there appeared to them tongues as of fire, distributed and resting on each one of them. And they were all filled with the Holy Spirit and began to speak in other tongues, as the Spirit gave them utterance.

Acts 2 vs. 2-4

Into the puny and fearful lives of those disciples the mighty power of God had come and they were impelled out into a hostile world to tell what great things God had done and to demonstrate by works of power that Christ was alive. I am utterly convinced that the same power of God's Holy Spirit is still available to all His people to-day. He can come in power into the life of every Christian and this He longs to do.

After Peter had experienced the infilling of the Holy Spirit he stood up to tell the wondering crowds what had happened to him and his companions. He explained that what they had experienced was the consequence of all that Christ had come to do. He had not only come into the world to set men free from sin and death but through His resurrection to raise all men who believe to new life too. Peter outlined the theology behind the gift they had just received.

> Being therefore exalted at the right hand of God, and having received from the Father the promise of the Holy Spirit, he has poured out this which you see and hear.
>
> Acts 2 v. 33

He went on to point out that the promise is not just for a 'chosen few' it is for all God's children.

> For the promise is to you and to your children and to all that are far off, every one whom the Lord our God calls to him.
>
> Acts 2 v. 39

There are many who read these texts to-day but because they cannot neatly tie the experience into their theological system are inclined to set it all aside. Those who think that way would do well to ponder some words of the Anglican theologian Michael Green. In his recent book *I believe in the Holy Spirit* he wrote:

> if the language which the neo-Pentecostals use for their experience is unfortunate, the same need not be the case with the experience itself. It is tragic that many Christians have robbed themselves of blessing because they distrusted, feared or despised this movement. They have been satisfied with a low level of spirituality. They have not allowed God to release them in prayer and praise and personal relationships, from the imprisonment of age-long inhibitions. They have not expected to see God at work in conversions,

in changing tough lives, in healing, in explicit guidance. They have forgotten that the manifestations of the Spirit in the New Testament had an uncomfortably concrete nature. Much of the division in the Churches that has come with the Pentecostals, has not been the fault of the Pentecostals themselves, but of the narrow, fearful, unspiritual Christianity in whose lukewarm waters many of us have for so long been willing to stay, terrified to launch out into the deep of experience of God. In an age when the Spirit of God is breaking up the fallow ground and the man-made barriers all over the world and irrespective of denomination, it would be ironic indeed if we missed what he has for us because we refused to get below the false linguistics in which the Pentecostals customarily express their living experience of God. Let those who want to retain the New Testament link between baptism in the Spirit and water baptism, justification, adoption—becoming a Christian in fact—make very sure that it is the full New Testament concept of baptism which they espouse; a plunging beneath the waters of the Spirit, an inundation with him, a vitality produced by him that could cause folk to wonder if we were drunk. Have we that power in prayer, that strength over temptation, that growing Christlikeness, which marked the communities of Christ in New Testament days and of which the one baptism was the outward bond?[1]

I have already said the phrase 'to be baptized in the Holy Spirit' is used in each of the four gospels in relation to Christ's work within us. Jesus Christ alone is the one who baptizes or immerses us in the Holy Spirit. In his very helpful theological examination of the whole issue in his book *Reflected Glory* Tom Smail gives this definition of 'baptism in the Spirit'.

> It is that aspect of Christian initiation in which, through expectant and appropriating faith in Christ's promises, the indwelling Holy Spirit manifests himself in our experience, so that he works in and through us with freedom and effectiveness, as he first worked with complete freedom and full effectiveness in the manhood of Christ.[2]

It was during a quiet retreat nearly four years ago that I entered into this experience in 'appropriating faith in Christ's promises'. A number of us in the University had been meeting regularly in the early mornings for prayer and to study the Acts of the Apostles. Towards the end of our time of study we spent a few days together to pray and think. During that time I became increasingly aware that all that Christ had won for me God was offering in the outpoured gift of His Holy Spirit. Undramatically though not without emotion I knelt in my room one evening and said 'Lord I thank you for what you have done and I gratefully receive what you are offering me'. In a sense before that I could say 'I had the Holy Spirit' for He lives in every believer. Now the Holy Spirit 'had me 'in a way that I was to experience in a thousand different expressions of His power working through me.

In trying to help others into this experience of 'receiving the power of God's Spirit' I often refer to the words of our Lord to Nicodemus when He said:

> The wind blows where it wills, and you hear the sound of it, but you do not know whence it

comes or whither it goes; so it is with every one who is born of the Spirit.

Saint John 3 v. 8

There is a deep mystery about God's dealings with an individual person. He created me. He loves each one of us with a deep and everlasting love. He longs that we should experience the fullness of His love and power flowing through our being. He wants us not only to know this with our head but with our heart.

> What father among you, if his son asks for a fish, will instead of a fish give him a serpent; or if he asks for an egg, will give him a scorpion? If you then, who are evil, know how to give good gifts to your children, how much more will the heavenly Father give the Holy Spirit to those who ask him!

Saint Luke 11 vs. 11-13

He gives His Holy Spirit in the fullness of His power not so much that we should experience a release of joy and peace and love in our own lives but more that we might be the channel of His presence and His power to others. The Holy Spirit always comes to glorify Jesus Christ. I remember a young graduate coming to see me after she had returned with her doctor husband from a tour of duty in East Africa. She and her husband had been greatly impressed by small groups of Spirit-filled Christians whom they had met right out in the bush. They had seen the power and the love of God manifest in the lives of those simple people. With tears in her eyes Hazel said to me: 'I want to be baptized in the Holy Spirit'. When I asked her why she wanted to be baptized in the Holy Spirit I shall never forget the answer she made. 'Because I want to be more aware of Jesus in my life'. And that is the main qualification.

Saint John records that at the Jewish Feast of Tabernacles Jesus stood up in the middle of the crowd and with a loud voice proclaimed:

> If any one thirst, let him come to me and drink.
> He who believes in me, as the scripture has said,
> Out of his heart shall flow rivers of living water.
>
> Saint John 7 vs. 37b and 38

Then John adds:

> Now this he said about the Spirit, which those who believed in him were to receive; for as yet the Spirit had not been given, because Jesus was not yet glorified.
>
> Saint John 7 v. 39

Jesus Christ is now glorified and seated at the right hand of the Father and the desire and prayer of His heart is that we should experience the overflowing power of His life and love.

This verse has been a great help to many people in appropriating the gift of the 'release of the Spirit'. The verbs which our Lord used are very significant. To thirst, to come, to drink and to believe. 'If any one thirst' God can only come to a life that is open to Him. He will not force His way into our lives, but when our hearts are filled with that longing for His presence and our souls are thirsty for His power then He longs to come.

> No ear may hear His coming
> , But in this world of sin,
> Where meek souls will receive Him, still,
> The dear Christ enters in.

If we are thirsty then we *come* to Christ the only one who is the source of 'living water' that will quench the soul's thirst and fully satisfy our deepest longings. When we come to Christ we must *drink.* I find there are many who stop short at this point in their quest for a new release of God's power. They thirst, they come to Jesus but they fail to drink. No one else can do this for me.

As Tom Smail so aptly puts it:

> Drinking is that obedience of faith which says the human 'yes' to God's promise and proceeds to act upon its truth. It does not have its source in itself or its value in itself but only in the word and presence of Christ. But faced with that word and in that presence it does not relapse into inactivity but reaches out and takes what is offered to it. [3]

Then Christ says to us believe. 'Believe now that what I have promised and what you have requested you now possess'. Faith is not based on my feelings but on the word and promise of Christ. When I receive the gift that Christ is freely offering me I thank Him with all my heart for what He has done. Saint John in his first Epistle puts it very clearly:

> And this is the confidence which we have in him, that if we ask anything according to his will he hears us. And if we know that he hears us in whatever we ask, we know that we have obtained the requests made of him.

1 John 5 vs. 14 and 15

We know by faith and then by the witness of the Spirit in our lives when 'out of our innermost being flow rivers of living water'. This text in Saint John chapter 7 v. 37 conjures up for me the picture of a fountain. Sometimes you come across a fountain that is completely dry. The structure is there but no water flows through. Sometimes you see a fountain and there is just a trickle of water flowing through. Frequently you see a fountain and fresh sparkling water is flowing from every exit.

So many Christian lives are like dried up fountains. We have all the right doctrines and the right language but

162

we lack that flow of living water that Christ promises as the inheritance of every believer. It is His purpose that every Christian should be so filled with the power of the Holy Spirit that the life of Christ is able to pour forth from us in unending benediction to the world around. It was surely an extravagant prayer which St. Paul prayed for the Ephesians "that they might be filled with all the fullness of God". These were no empty words which the Apostle prayed. He knew this should be their experience, and ours too. When I come in faith and self surrender to the Lord who loves me and has taken away my sins I can with confidence pray in the words of an anonymous writer.

> Thine is the throne-room of the soul!
> Its Ruler, break each barrier down;
> As with full tide o'erflood the whole,
> Self overborne by Thee alone . . .
> Spirit of truth, of holiness,
> We cry not 'enter', but 'possess.'

[1] *I Believe in the Holy Spirit* by Michael Green. Page 146, Hodder and Stoughton 1975.

[2] *Reflected Glory* by Thomas Smail. Page 141. Hodder and Stoughton 1975.

[3] *Reflected Glory* by Thomas Smail. Page 151. Hodder and Stoughton 1975.

For Your Meditation

Yet even now, says the Lord, return to me with all your heart, with fasting, with weeping, and with mourning; and rend your hearts and not your garments. Return to the Lord, your God, for he is gracious and merciful, slow to anger, and abounding in steadfast love, and repents of evil. Who knows whether he will not turn and repent, and leave a blessing behind him, a cereal offering and a drink offering for the Lord, your God? Blow the trumpet in Zion; sanctify a fast; call a solemn assembly; gather the people. Sanctify the congregation; assemble the elders; gather the children, even nursing infants. Let the bridegroom leave his room, and the bride her chamber. Between the vestibule and the altar let the priests, the ministers of the Lord, weep and say, Spare thy people, O Lord, and make not thy heritage a reproach, a byword among the nations. Why should they say among the peoples, 'Where is their God?'

And it shall come to pass afterward, that I will pour out my spirit on all flesh; your sons and your daughters shall prophesy, your old men shall dream dreams, and your young men shall see visions. Even upon the menservants and maidservants in those days, I will pour out my spirit.   Joel 2 vs. 12-17, 28 and 29

A Prayer

For this reason I bow my knees before the Father, from whom every family in heaven and on earth is named, that according to the riches of his glory he may grant you to be strengthened with might through his Spirit in the inner man, and that Christ may dwell in your hearts through faith; that you, being rooted and grounded in love, may have power to comprehend with all the saints what is the breadth and length and height and depth, and to know the love of Christ which surpasses knowledge, that you may be filled with all the fullness of God. Now to him who by the power at work within us is able to do far more abundantly than all that we ask or think, to him be glory in the church and in Christ Jesus to all generations, for ever and ever. Amen.

Ephesians 3 vs. 14-21

Acknowledgements

Grateful acknowledgement is made to Ave Maria Press for the quotation from Ralph Martin's *Unless the Lord Build the House;*

to Darton, Longman and Todd for the quotation from Cardinal Suenens' *A New Pentecost?;*

to Christian Publications Inc. for the quotation from A. W. Tozer's *The Pursuit of God;*

to Fontana Books for the quotation from Martin Luther King's *Strength to Love* and from J. B. Phillips' *The Young Church in Action;*

to Gill & Macmillan for the quotation from Michael Quoist's *Christ is Alive;*

to Hodder & Stoughton for the quotations from Michael Green's *Evangelism in the Early Church* and *I Believe in the Holy Spirit* and from Thomas Smail's *Reflected Glory;*

to S.C.M. Press for quotations from John V. Taylor's *The Go Between God* and from Lesslie Newbigin's *The Household of God* and from A. M. Ramsey's & L-J. Suenens' *The Future of the Church;*

to Tyndale Press for the quotation from John B. Taylor's commentary on *Ezekiel;*

to Word of Life Books for the quotation from Vinson Synan's *Charismatic Bridges;*

to the Division of Education of the National Council of Churches of Christ in the USA for the quotations from the *Revised Standard Version;*

and to J. B. Phillips for the quotations from *The New Testament in Modern English.*